Dedication

To my Gram,

Your love for God and His Word has always been real for you, which has helped make it real for me.

Your legacy to me has been to always personalize your favorite verse: Isaiah 41:10, "Fear not, *Sherrie*, for I am with *you*. Be not dismayed, *Sherrie*, for I am *your* God; I will strengthen *you*, I will help *you*, I will uphold *you* with my righteous right hand."

You know God loves you. He is your friend, companion, help, and refuge.

Thank you for how you have impacted me. I can certainly look at your life of more than 100 years and say...

"*Oh, what a life!*"

4

Contents

Introduction

I will never forget the night I had a "conversation" with God. It was not an audible conversation, and I did not have any visions, but I knew God wanted me to learn something. It was several years ago at a concert of one of my favorite female vocalists. I was excited for the performance, but I did not expect God to use this concert to change my perspective on all of life itself.

Before I go further, I should explain how important and powerful music is for me. Music has always been a big part of my life. My family sang everywhere—in the car, in church, around the campfire, washing dishes, and family get-togethers—you get the picture: we sang all the time. Music is also a big part of my salvation testimony, and it continues to be significant in my life. So I am not surprised that God chose a concert to teach me something huge about my life.

We were on the main level about halfway back. The rows were packed, and the atmosphere was coursing with excitement and energy. I watched as she sang—she was extremely musically gifted, but there was something more. She was overflowing right there on stage, singing, expressing, pouring from her very core. It was beautiful. I was moved not only by what she was saying, but also by how she was saying it.

That is when it happened. The Holy Spirit was moving in my heart, and I sure felt it. If it had been a real, face-to-face conversation, I imagine it would have gone something like this:

ME: *Oh Father, this is so beautiful! Look how she expresses. I love music and I want to express, too. Won't you please let me sing like that?*

GOD: *No, Sherrie. Singing is not what you do.*

ME: *I know I don't do it like this God, but You could make me. You can help me.*

GOD: *No, Sherrie. I haven't made you to sing.*

ME: *But look at how she can express to You and to those around her how much she loves you!*

GOD: *Uh-huh.*

ME: *That's what I want to do. I love You and want to express it like that.*

GOD: *So what's stopping you? I made you to teach. Why not do it in your teaching?*

God was trying to tell me that I could make a difference; I could express all my heart wanted to say and help others know that He was my deepest passion. But I did not need to be a singer to do it. I needed to do it right where He had placed me. Now, that is exactly what I hope to do.

Life is Meant to be Lived!

Life should be an expression—an overflow—of His life in me. That is what God has placed me here for, right? To help others see Him and understand who He is. So what am I waiting for? I waste so much time just existing, hoping for the better life I've always dreamed of rather than actually living the life God has given me. He has not placed us here to just tolerate or survive but rather to thrive. Autopilot is not real living.

The good news is that neither you nor I have to be stuck in lives of non-responsiveness. There is hope! We can have meaningful, purposeful lives. Jesus had a conversation with a woman who was living on autopilot. She struggled to find answers until she met Someone who asked her the right questions. She needed hope for her future, but also for her present life. He told her:

> *"Whoever drinks of the water that I will give him will never be thirsty again. The water that I will give him will become in him a spring of water welling up to eternal life."* John 4:14

The life God intends us to live should be more like a wellspring than a puddle of muddy water. There IS hope. We do not have to live in thirst!

Looking Ahead

This book will not provide the latest and greatest "Five easy steps to..." You and I both know those do not really exist, although we secretly wish they did. I want to show you that you really do have a life worth living.

In the first section, we will look at what Paul wrote to the church in Ephesus (that is the book of Ephesians) about the extent of God's work in his life. We must understand our need for the gospel—both before and after salvation—to truly understand the appropriate response to who He is and what He has done.

Paul later wrote to another church (the Corinthians) to help them see what an appropriate response—a lifestyle—would look like in their lives. There are a few principles there to grab onto that will help us understand what living should look like in daily reality.

It is not a rule book or a to-do list. It is called abundant life, and it is what Jesus Christ came to provide. I do not think we should wait for Heaven to begin living it.

> *"I am the door. If anyone enters by me, he will be saved and will go in and out and find pasture. The thief comes only to steal and kill and destroy. I came that they may have life and have it abundantly."*
> John 10:9–10

We will be studying in the English Standard Version of the Bible throughout the book. I like this version, and it is the one I use the most while studying and teaching.

If you get nothing else out of this book, I hope you understand two things: first, God loves you with an extraordinary love. Second, real living is possible, and it is in response to understanding who God is and His love for you.

I am glad you have joined me. The journey is one that will continue for each of us until we see Jesus. So how about it? Are you ready to start LIVING!?!

Sherrie Holloway
Wellspring

Acknowledgments

Through 20 years of coaching, I learned many things, and one of those definitely applies here—a project like this takes many hands and even more brains! This book is the result of many servants doing what God has wired them to do best. I am grateful for their labors, encouragement, feedback, corrections, and friendship. I have heard the phrase, "It is hard to find good help these days," but I will attest that it is not impossible because I have found some of the best.

Thank you to my family, who though they know me most, continue to encourage me and pray for me in this process. God has blessed me with a godly heritage, and I never want to take the impact it had for granted. Your prayers and encouragement along the way have meant much, and I am grateful God chose to put us together!

The process of taking my speaking sessions and notes and putting them in chapters is due much to the work of Emily Gehman. Thank you for joining this journey. Who knew joining me at a speaking engagement one weekend would have led to this? You did a wonderful job, and it is a pleasure working with you.

I am blessed with people in my life I call "balcony people"—those who believe in me and cheer me on. Among those is a good friend and this project's manager, Dena Cambra. Thank you for using your expertise, your smarts, your abilities, and your belief in this project and in me to see this through to the end. I do not think I would have started this if it were not for you setting up that first meeting. Thank you for continuing to be my friend through all of it.

Thanks to Kathy Compton, Dawn Jacobs, Beth Welman, Christie Lothamer, Amber Severance, Martha Bolton, Mel Walker, Dr. Jim Lytle, and Sharon Weigle who gave their "two cents" and added greatly with layout, editing skills, and good old-fashioned opinions and advice. I am indebted to those who worked so meticulously to make sure the wording and appearance worked together to give a single message. Thank you. I am a better person because of your part in my life, and this is a better book because of your part in it.

The passion in me for the Word began when I was a student at Baptist Bible College in Pennsylvania. It was there I learned to think, ask good questions, and study the Bible. It was the revelation of my God and His plan, and I wanted to know more about both. I am so thankful for those professors who poured into my life as a student in the classroom and a player on the basketball court. They instilled a love for God, His Word, and life itself. Jim Lytle, Joe Schloegel, Nancy Durrwachter…I am who I am today because of your continued investment. Thank you.

My passion to live has developed over the years by rubbing shoulders with those who enjoyed life and want even more of it. I found some of those friends at BBC as a student and as a professor and coach. Beth, Christie, Michelle, Jen—to each of you: thank you for your friendship. Let's keep on living!

Above all, I want to humbly thank my God for loving me and giving me new life. It is only through His grace, power, and direction that living is worthwhile. I am thankful to have His name and want to live each day in a way that helps others see just how great He is.

For the Love of God

Chapter 1

Girl, You Need Jesus!

He loves me! He loves me not. He loves me! He loves me not. He loves me! He loves me not. He loves me—I think I will stop there.

Ah, the amazing power of a daisy. Ever since this French game began in the nineteenth century, people have been asking daisies to reveal whether or not their affection toward an individual is returned. Sounds pretty silly, doesn't it—asking a daisy about love as though it has some special power? Strange. We all know daisies cannot show us anything about love. But we want love so badly we will do almost anything to try and find it.

Psychology tells us that everyone has three basic needs: love, security, and significance. One of our very foundational needs is to be loved! I agree with that. Do you? Does it surprise you at all? Perhaps you have never asked a daisy about love, but chances are you *have* wondered if you were loved. There may have been times when you felt invisible or unimportant to the world, or even worse, to those closest to you. Love is a basic human need; when we are not sure we are loved, it is a bit unsettling.

But maybe it is not just about being loved. Maybe it is more about understanding that you *are* loved. *Your* need for love is met. *My* need for love is met. But unfortunately, you do not always feel that way. When feelings run the show, the search for love begins. You look in places that cannot provide what your heart really needs or longs for. Sometimes the search includes people; sometimes it includes circumstances, or shopping…or food…or…(Right?) But none of these things, even if you acquired all of them, would meet the need for love. They would not help you understand that you *are* loved.

As a single woman, there are times when I have a real sense of the "missing person" in my life. Yet if God does give me a husband, that man will still never be able to fulfill that deepest need. I was created, and *you were created* for something more than any human relationship can supply. You were created for intimate relationship on the deepest level—a relationship with the One who made you and knows you best: God Himself.

Have you ever thought there is more to life than this? Have you ever felt as though there was something missing? Some*one* missing?

We spend much of our time looking for love in tangible ways—ones that are so readily available in our society today. Yet, when we find them, we have an even greater sense of need and are emptier than before. The truth is, you can only find what your soul craves in a relationship with God. Without this relationship, you are dead spiritually. With a relationship with God, you are alive spiritually. He makes you alive. He gives purpose for life.

Stop Searching, Start Living
You would think that, for a human who is still breathing and has a pulse and brain activity, living is a piece of cake. By the physiological definition of "life," that *is* living, or at least being alive. But what does it mean to live—*really* live?

We are missing out, but we have become so busy, we do not even notice. God never intended for you to be satisfied with mere existence. He does not want you to miss what He is doing in, through, and for you because you are too busy. You have been tricked into thinking that life is only as good as how full the calendar is. You hit the autopilot button, get everything done, and then wonder, *what did I actually do today?*

We often find ourselves active or involved, but we are not connected. We live, talk, move, do, finish, etc. without thinking and spend days, weeks, months, or even years without any real purpose.

We use phrases like "going through the motions," "busy," or "checked out." (Sometimes I even forget to check IN!) The disconnect happens when we are not living intentionally, when we are not purposefully aware of our thoughts and choices.

You have experienced this before. Have you ever put the milk in the pantry and the cereal in the refrigerator? Or have you done something out of order in your normal routine and then did not know what to do next? When I moved into my house, I had to turn right at an intersection instead of left on my way home from work. I knew where I lived, but there were many days I turned left instead of right. There was a disconnect, which happens even in our daily lives because we are just not paying attention. We slide into "neutral" instead of "drive."

> *Real living is first understanding God's real love and then responding to it.*

There is a lot more to living than just the physiological requirements of respiration, pulse, and brain activity, although those are very important. Living is actually a response. We live in response to the love of God. *That* is real love. But you cannot respond to what you do not know or believe. If you cannot respond, then you cannot live. Just stop for a moment and let that sink in. *If you cannot respond, then you cannot live.* Real living is not a new program or technique; it is first understanding God's real love and then responding to it.

Real love begins with the gospel. So that is where we are going to start.

Read It for Yourself

We are going to spend the majority of Part One of this book in Ephesians 2:1–10. I have included it here for you to read; it will show up again and again in the next few chapters. This is key to our study, because it is God's Word that changes hearts. Nothing I could write has life–changing capability. Every part of Scripture is used to shape, train, and equip us for the glory of God. Paul was writing to his friend, Timothy, when he said this:

> *"[16]All Scripture is breathed out by God and profitable for teaching, for reproof, for correction, and for training in righteousness, [17]that the man of God may be competent, equipped for every good work."* 2 Timothy 3:16–17

That is why this book will include Scripture so frequently. Spend some time in Ephesians 2 right now. No need to rush. Just read it and allow it to soak in. We will unpack it in the coming pages.

> *"[1]And you were dead in the trespasses and sins [2]in which you once walked, following the course of this world, following the prince of the power of the air, the spirit that is now at work in the sons of disobedience—[3]among whom we all once lived in the passions of our flesh, carrying out the desires of the body and the mind, and were by nature children of wrath, like the rest of mankind. [4]But God, being rich in mercy, because of the great love with which He*

loved us, ⁵even when we were dead in our trespasses, made us alive together with Christ—by grace you have been saved—⁶and raised us up with Him and seated us with Him in the heavenly places in Christ Jesus, ⁷so that in the coming ages He might show the immeasurable riches of His grace in kindness toward us in Christ Jesus. ⁸For by grace you have been saved through faith. And this is not your own doing; it is the gift of God, ⁹not a result of works, so that no one may boast. ¹⁰For we are His workmanship, created in Christ Jesus for good works, which God prepared beforehand, that we should walk in them." Ephesians 2:1–10

That, my friends, is the gospel—the wonderful truth of God's love toward a sin–filled person like me (and you). From the very beginning, God had a plan to rescue you from the sin that had trapped you. That plan included Him showing His love in a very tangible way. See it there in the middle of the passage? *"But God, being rich in mercy, because of the great love with which He loved us, even when we were dead in our trespasses, made us alive together with Christ…"*

You were dead because of sin. But because of God's love and mercy, He sent Jesus Christ to come and make you alive. That is the gospel, and it is where you begin a new life. It is where you must remain.

It Is For Everyone

Paul is not writing to unbelievers in Ephesians 2. He is writing to the church in Ephesus. The letter is for believers. He is preaching the gospel. We know the readers are believers because at the beginning of the letter in his greeting, Paul addresses it to "believers" or "brothers" or "saints" in the particular region to which he is writing.

Paul thinks this—the gospel—is pretty important, because we find in almost every one of his letters a similar gospel portion. Here are some other places Paul presents the gospel to believers:

Letter	Gospel Text
Romans 5:8	"...God shows his love for us in that while we were still sinners, Christ died for us."
1 Corinthians 15:3–4	"³...Christ died for our sins in accordance with the Scriptures, ⁴that He was buried, that He was raised on the third day in accordance with the Scriptures..."
2 Corinthians 5:14–15	"¹⁴...that One has died for all, therefore all have died; ¹⁵and He died for all, that those who live might no longer live for themselves but for Him who for their sake died and was raised."
Galatians 2:16	"...a person is not justified by works of the law but through faith in Jesus Christ, so we also have believed in Christ Jesus, in order to be justified by faith in Christ and not by works of the law..."
Philippians 2:7–8	"⁷but made himself nothing, taking the form of a servant, being born in the likeness of men. ⁸And being found in human form, he humbled himself by becoming obedient to the point of death, even death on a cross."
Colossians 1:19–20	"¹⁹For in Him all the fullness of God was pleased to dwell, ²⁰and through Him to reconcile to Himself all things, whether on earth or in Heaven, making peace by the blood of His cross."
1 Thessalonians 5:9–10	"⁹For God has not destined us for wrath, but to obtain salvation through our Lord Jesus Christ, ¹⁰who died for us so that whether we are awake or asleep we might live with Him."
2 Thessalonians 2:13–14	"¹³But we ought always to give thanks to God for you, brothers beloved by the Lord, because God chose you as the firstfruits to be saved, through sanctification by the Spirit and belief in the truth. ¹⁴To this He called you through our gospel, so that you may obtain the glory of our Lord Jesus Christ."

Letter	Gospel Text
1 Timothy 2:5–6	"⁵For there is one God, and there is one mediator between God and men, the man Christ Jesus, ⁶who gave Himself as a ransom for all, which is the testimony given at the proper time."
2 Timothy 1:10	"...our Savior Christ Jesus, who abolished death and brought life and immortality to light through the gospel."
Titus 2:13–14	"¹³...our great God and Savior Jesus Christ, ¹⁴Who gave Himself for us to redeem us from all lawlessness and to purify for Himself a people for His own possession who are zealous for good works."

Where did we get this idea that the gospel is only for unbelievers? Clearly we did not get it from the Scriptures. The gospel is written throughout the pages of Scripture. For some reason, we think that after we are saved, we are done with the gospel.

But we are wrong. We do need the gospel. John Piper, theologian, veteran pastor, and author puts it this way:

"What's the gospel? I will put it in a sentence. The gospel is the news that Jesus Christ, the Righteous One, died for our sins and rose again, eternally triumphant over all his enemies, so that there is now no condemnation for those who believe, but only everlasting joy. That is the gospel. You never, never, never outgrow your need for it. Do not ever think of the gospel as 'That is the way you get saved, and then you get strong by leaving it and doing something else.' No! We are strengthened by God through the gospel every day, till the day we drop. You never outgrow the need to preach to yourself the gospel."[1]

You see, *we need the gospel.* You and I need the gospel every day. Whether it is the first time you have heard it or the

---

[1] http://www.desiringgod.org/resource–library/articles/the–Gospel–in–6–minutes

783,624th time you have heard it. We are forgetful creatures, and we need to be reminded of the gospel. We need it.

You will never, ever outgrow your need for the gospel. You will never reach a point when you do not need to be reminded of Christ's work of love. It is not going to happen. When you forget that you are loved, how you live says there is no hope or joy. You need to be reminded.

When I first understood my need in a church pew about forty years ago, it was very evident to me that I needed God. I could not do anything to get to heaven, but He loved me so much that He provided the way. Too many times, I forget about my desperate need. I try to turn life and growth into a checklist of accomplishments instead of the process of God's work in me. When I see myself "getting better," my need for the gospel diminishes in comparison. If I am "getting better," I need Him less.

You will never, ever outgrow your need for the gospel.

Instead, my growth should show me just how needy I am, how powerful sin's grip is, and how incapable I am of any good by myself. My need for the gospel should grow as my understanding grows.

As I write this chapter, my Gram is struggling physically. Gram has lived across the street from my family since I was five (I try not to think about how long ago that was). There is one thing I know to be true about my Gram—she loves Jesus. Though her mind is slipping now, I have watched her for many years. She talks about growing up and how hard it was for her, tells stories about the night she and my grandfather eloped, vacations, family memories, and a host of other things. Every story usually begins and/or ends with something like, "God has been so good to me."

She sits in a rehab facility now. This past year she has broken both hips and shattered her elbow; she has come close to death because of pneumonia and heart failure, but still she says, "God has been so good to me." What is it in someone that would enable her to say that and actually mean it? It is because she understands her need—not just now because she is 100 years old (yes, 100!), and her health is failing, but because she operated with that understanding throughout life. When her husband of 62 years and 5 months (that is how she always says it) died, when financial problems came, when life was free of hardships, when she gives time to help, when she crochets another blanket for someone, whatever the circumstances, she resolved never to move from the truth that God is good, and she needs Him.

Sometimes I am reminded of my need for the gospel when I am driving and no one else on the road seems to understand my schedule, or when I am dealing with a student who is hearing the same speech about homework for the third time. I needed the gospel when I heard the person on the phone telling me my brother had cancer, or when I had to explain to my players that after twenty years of coaching, this would be my last with them. I need the gospel when life is just plain hard, lonely, or sad, or—you fill in the blank. I even need the gospel when God's blessings are evident, like when he provided me with the perfect house, or when we celebrated Gram's 100th birthday.

Hard, easy, sad, joyful, whatever life is throwing at me, I am dependent on what God is doing in me, for me, and through me. I cannot do it alone. He must do it, and I must learn to willingly submit to His work.

I am sure you can make your own list of ups and downs:

❉ You just lost your job.

❉ You just got married, and life has not turned out like you thought it would.

❉ No one asked you to be that special someone.

❉ Your son or daughter is on a tour of duty in the military.

❉ Someone just gave you a car!

❉ Your spouse has been unfaithful.

❉ You have been called to a new ministry.

❉ A weather disaster wreaked havoc on your home.

❉ Your first grandbaby is on its way!

❉ Your child makes decisions you were not prepared for.

❉ You melt your favorite skirt with the iron (yes, I really did that!).

❉ You got a new job doing what you love!

❉ The car has a flat tire on the freeway.

❉ You get injured before the sports season begins.

The way you respond to these joys and heartaches reveals what you believe and how deeply it has penetrated your heart. Living in response to God's love gives you a bigger-picture view of your circumstances. While sometimes it might not take the sting out of a particular situation, it provides the hope that is often hard to find in those *what-in-the-world?* moments. You will face disappointments and challenges beyond your capabilities, but the truth that God loves you and made you His own should give a security beyond anything you could ever have. Hard times remind you of your need for Him; the celebrated moments of life drive you back to God's provision and grace.

The gospel—the truth of God's love that was displayed in Jesus' sacrifice for the entire past, present, and future world— is the reason we have hope. It is the reason we have purpose. It is the reason we can live fully engaged, and THAT IS why we need it.

Faith in the gospel of Jesus Christ does not just sign you up for eternal life, although that is a pretty amazing benefit. You do not have to wait until Heaven to start living an incredible life. Jesus proclaimed it Himself:

> *"⁹I am the door. If anyone enters by me, he will be saved and will go in and out and find pasture. ¹⁰The thief comes only to steal and kill and destroy. I came that they may have life and have it abundantly."*
> John 10:9–10

Paul talked about it in another letter to the Thessalonians:

> *"⁹For God has not destined us for wrath, but to obtain salvation through our Lord Jesus Christ, ¹⁰who died for us so that whether we are awake or asleep we might live with Him."* 1 Thessalonians 5:9–10

So that is where we are going to start: the gospel. Why? Because we *need* the gospel. Girl, you need Jesus! It is He who enables you to click the switch off autopilot and engage in real living. Abundant living.

Through the pages of Scripture, God says that cruising through life without thinking, without engaging, is boring (and exhausting). It does not take long to figure that out. But it does not have to be that way. Real living is possible no matter the situation you find yourself in. This real living happens because of, and in response to, who God is and knowing that *you are loved.* So let's get started with the gospel. Here, God's love is found to be incomparable to any other kind. By the end of Part One, you will be shouting, "Oh, what a love!"

Personal Reflection

If your "love tank" had a gauge, what would it read right now?

What is it that you turn to for love? Is it working?

What are the consequences of being disconnected in your personal daily life?

Do you realize God's love for you through Jesus Christ? If you have accepted Christ as your Savior, take time to write out your testimony and thank God for His work in your life.

If you have never accepted Christ, why not? Take time to write down some thoughts, doubts, or concerns that are keeping you from Christ.

Think about what is going on in your life—your roles, responsibilities, relationships, needs, etc. What do you need the gospel for right now?

For the Love of God

Chapter 2

"How ever could one know what sweetness is
If one had never tasted bitterness?
For inward happiness was never his
Who never was in sorrow or distress."

Troilus and Criseyde, Geoffrey Chaucer[2]

Dead Woman Walking

Severe weather and natural disasters have a way of reminding me how fortunate I am. I have a tendency to take little, yet very major things for granted every day. When a powerful storm whisks its way through my part of the country it is likely that some will lose power. The winds, rain, snow, and ice can cripple an entire city. As I write, we sit in the wake of a "superstorm" that wreaked havoc on the eastern coastline. Millions of people had to live without electricity, water, or heat for days and some for weeks. It is times like these that help us understand just how reliant we are on those utilities. We pay the bill each month, flip on the lights, turn up the heat, make dinner, take a warm shower, and think nothing of it—until it is gone. Understanding just how hard life is without these amenities gives us a better appreciation for them.

In a very similar way, we gain a better understanding of our salvation and what we have if we get a glimpse of just how

---

[2] Chaucer, Geoffrey, and Nevill Coghill. *Troilus and Criseyde*. Harmondsworth: Penguin, 1971. Print.

terrible life is without Christ and what He has made available for us. To understand life, we must first understand death.

Paul does this when he begins chapter two of his letter to the people in Ephesus. He wants them to understand where they came from so that they might be able to respond to what God has done.

The Who

So let's dive into the text headfirst. Get your pen or pencil out; we are going to do some marking. I officially give you permission to write in this book!

First, read the entire portion of Scripture printed here for you. On your mark, get set...Go!

> "¹And you were dead in the trespasses and sins ²in which you once walked, following the course of this world, following the prince of the power of the air, the spirit that is now at work in the sons of disobedience—³among whom we all once lived in the passions of our flesh, carrying out the desires of the body and the mind, and were by nature children of wrath, like the rest of mankind. ⁴But God, being rich in mercy, because of the great love with which He loved us, ⁵even when we were dead in our trespasses, made us alive together with Christ—by grace you have been saved—⁶and raised us up with Him and seated us with Him in the heavenly places in Christ Jesus, ⁷so that in the coming ages He might show the immeasurable riches of His grace in kindness toward us in Christ Jesus. ⁸For by grace you have been saved through faith. And this is not your own doing; it is the gift of God, ⁹not a result of works, so that no one may boast. ¹⁰For we are His workmanship, created in Christ Jesus for good works, which God prepared

beforehand, that we should walk in them." Ephesians
2:1–10

Are you ready? Your first task is to circle the second word of
the passage.

That word shows exactly who Paul is writing about. Do you
see it?

You. Yes, you. He is writing to you. Well, okay, He is writing
to the Ephesians. But guess what? The characteristics Paul
says are true about the Ephesians are also true about you and
me. We are in the same condition as the people in Ephesus.

The What

Still have your pen or pencil? Okay. Your next task: circle the
fourth word in the passage. What did you find? Write it here:

The word that describes your condition is dead. Dead.

You are familiar with death, its unexpectedness, its cruelty on
your emotions, and the mourning it brings. But even though
you know death, sometimes you do not "get it." You really do
not understand dead. It is the difference
between seeing a dead dog and a dog
playing dead. One is repulsive; the other
is cute. How is that possible? You do not
get it.

*You will never, ever
outgrow your need
for the gospel.*

Being dead implies an emptiness and lack
of life. It is not just about not existing.
It is about an incredible void of everything. Along with this
emptiness there is a total, complete helplessness. When you
are dead, you cannot do anything, and you remain in this
state because you are dead. You are unable to get yourself
what you need most—life.

Death is an all-or-nothing situation. You cannot be half-dead
or partially dead or almost dead; there are no degrees of

deadness. You are either dead or alive. No middle ground. No gray area. Dead or alive.

But in Ephesians 2, Paul is not talking about physical death. He is talking about spiritual death, and it is this realm that we need to be paying attention to. While I do not want to be morbid here, we do need to discuss this problem of being spiritually dead.

The Greek word used in the New Testament for "dead" is *nekros*.[3] That probably does not mean much to you, but I want to point out something about this Greek word. There are two different uses of the word. The first is its proper use, describing the physical void of life: deceased, departed, and destitute of life. The second is the use of the metaphor of spiritual death: unable to do right, predisposed to sin, and destitute of real life.

It is the same word used for both ideas.

So what?

Let me explain. In the Greek language in which the New Testament was originally crafted, there will often be more than one Greek word or idea for a concept, but in English, it only translates into one word. For example, in the Greek culture and language, there were three distinct concepts of love: *eros*, *agape*, and *phileo*.[4] Each word describes a different kind of love; we only have one broad idea of love. There is a similar occurrence with our word "discipline." There are actually five Greek words for "discipline," each one used differently.[5]

But for this word, "dead," there is only one Greek word: *nekros*. There is not another word Paul can use to differentiate

---

[3] www.blueletterbible.org/lang/lexicon/lexicon.cfm?Strongs=G3498&t=KJV

[4] James R. Lytle, D.Min. Interview. March 23, 2013.

[5] http://www.preceptaustin.org/greek_word_studies1.htm

between physical death and any other kind of death, even though the idea can describe many different situations.

Again, so what? Keep reading.

Paul has to use the only word there is: *nekros*. A word that conjures up thoughts of sorrow, ugliness, and lifelessness. A word that makes stomachs turn, hopes fall, and hearts long for more. This word is powerful, and Paul wants it that way. It compels the reader to make a deeper connection.

Paul means business when he talks about spiritual death. He could have used a lighter term or described it as a metaphor. But he did not say, "You were like dead people." No. He said, "You were dead people." No metaphor. Actual death.

Yeah, so?

This is serious. This is not just Paul trying to make a point by exaggerating. This is Paul speaking truth.

Death is real. Physical death is real, and spiritual death is real. They both have major consequences, which began in the Garden of Eden. When Adam and Eve chose to disobey God, their sin introduced to mankind both physical and spiritual death. The consequences of spiritual death, however, are much more devastating than those of physical death. Do not miss that. As awful as physical death is, spiritual death is worse. Let me explain.

When God created Adam and Eve, their physical bodies were perfect. They came with a longer-than-lifetime guarantee. But their disobedience had consequences in the physical realm that destroyed the perfection of their bodies, and they could no longer live forever. Their bodies were going to wear out and would eventually die. The account of the fall of man given in Genesis shows us exactly what God said to the couple after they had sinned. Take a look:

> *"By the sweat of your face you shall eat bread, till*
> *you return to the ground, for out of it you were*
> *taken; for you are dust, and to dust you shall return."*
> Genesis 3:19

As I mentioned earlier, my Gram is 100 years old and has been through quite a bit in her lifetime, as you can imagine. Just the past few years include a broken arm, two fractured hips, a shattered elbow, pneumonia, and congestive heart failure—just to name a few. There have been several times when we thought her time here on earth was ending, but she is still here. I joke that she has nine lives and is now on number fifteen! But the reality is, she will not live forever. Eventually her body will give out. She will not be on this earth forever, and neither will we. Sometimes we forget that.

Our sin separates us from God.

No one is immune to physical death, even my Gram. Physical death is a common predicament.

But physical death is the least of your worries. Spiritual death is even worse.

After that first sin in the Garden of Eden, Adam and Eve never again had the same kind of relationship with God. The couple felt shame where once there had been intimacy with the Lord; their sin had come between them and God. We know this because of their change in behavior after their sin. Before, Adam and Eve walked with God in the garden and enjoyed open communication, but after they chose to disobey, they hid from God.

> *"And they heard the sound of the LORD God*
> *walking in the garden in the cool of the day, and the*
> *man and his wife hid themselves from the presence*

of the Lord among the trees of the garden." Genesis 3:8

Not only did they lose the open communication, but they lost the privilege to live in the place God had made for them to enjoy. They were cut off from the Garden, the place where they communed with God daily.

"²³...therefore the LORD God sent him out from the garden of Eden to work the ground from which he was taken. ²⁴He drove out the man, and at the east of the garden of Eden He placed the cherubim and a flaming sword that turned every way to guard the way to the tree of life." Genesis 3:23–24

I would like to tell you that after Adam and Eve's sin, they learned their lesson and it stopped there. But I cannot because it did not stop there.

The fall into sin created an effect that the entire world experiences. It brought a curse on the world that renders every person ever born sinful, spiritually dead, and desperately estranged from God. Paul says it this way in his letter to the Romans:

"Therefore, just as sin came into the world through one man, and death through sin, and so death spread to all men because all sinned." Romans 5:12

This is our greatest problem. Our sin separates us from God. He is not just a more than above average human being that we are trying to impress or earn love from. God is above humanness. He is righteous, perfect, and holy. Because of our sin, we cannot enjoy God or be in His presence like Adam and Eve did in the Garden of Eden. Spiritual death creates a chasm between us and God that we can never cross on our own. As long as we are dead, we will never, ever experience Him like we were created to.

> *"...for all have sinned and fall short of the glory of God..."* Romans 3:23

Spiritual death spares no one. Every single one of us enters the world physically alive but spiritually dead. It is our original status.

Let me be blunt. You are spiritually dead. You entered this world physically alive but spiritually dead. Sin dictates that your preexisting condition is spiritual deadness. There is nothing you can do about it, and you are left in a sad state of affairs.

Helpless and Hopeless

I hate to be the bearer of bad news, but your condition leaves you weak, powerless, and without a ray of hope. You are totally without God and incapable of finding Him, because when you are dead, you are dead.

You are unable to do anything in and of yourself. You cannot move, you cannot breathe, you cannot talk, listen, sing, pray, or love. You are inadequate, unable, incapable, lifeless, breathless, extinct, limp, exhausted. You have no hope.

The sin that Adam and Eve fell into became a problem for your entire existence, and you now carry a nature that is drenched in sin. Sin dictates everything you do. You can try and do good, but there is no good in you. Sometimes you can do things that look good to the world, but because God knows your heart, they do not look so good to Him. Sin determines the way you live.

Paul describes what spiritual death looks like as he continues in the passage. Take a look and underline the phrases that describe what spiritual death produces.

> *"¹And you were dead in the trespasses and sins*
> *²in which you once walked, following the course*

> *of this world, following the prince of the power of
> the air, the spirit that is now at work in the sons of
> disobedience—³among whom we all once lived in the
> passions of our flesh, carrying out the desires of the
> body and the mind, and were by nature children of
> wrath, like the rest of mankind."* Ephesians 2:1–3

In your own words, describe what it means to "walk in
trespasses and sins." Paul says dead people walk in sin. Dead
people cannot go anywhere or do anything apart from sin. It
is sin, deadness that is in control.

Paul talks about "sons of disobedience." What does he say the
sons of disobedience do?

We "follow the prince of the power of the air." By God's
permission, Satan has power in our depraved, sinful
world. He is the one who has authority over "the sons of
disobedience," who choose to disobey God. Sin—spiritual
death—binds us in slavery to Satan, making us sons of
disobedience. It says we all lived like that. We followed "the
passions of our flesh." We did whatever we wanted to do, and
because of our sinful nature, that was always sin.

All of this made us "children of wrath, just like the rest
of mankind." The entire human race is bound to these
characteristics. Mankind is spiritually dead and desperately
sinful. And there is nothing we can do about it.

According to verses 1–3, what does it mean to be spiritually
dead?

Rewrite verses 1–3 in your own words.

Spiritual death. It is not a pretty picture, but in order to fully appreciate God's great salvation, you have to understand how great your sin is. Left to yourself, you are helpless and hopeless. That is the bad news. But the good news is that you have not been left to yourself.

Personal Reflection

In your own words, write a definition of "death."

What are some of your "trespasses and sins"?

In our sin, we are helpless and hopeless. What other words can you use to describe your situation?

For the Love of God

Chapter 3

The Biggest "But" of Your Life

The world of cinema has taken full advantage of the power of music. The music in a movie grabs viewers and brings them into the story. I am guessing you have experienced this before. You have become part of the team that discovers a hidden hallway or cautiously makes its way through the unknown forest. The music has helped pull you in. The low strings set the mood for mystery or suspense; the brass and strings in a minor key accompany the villain's entrance; and the major keys bring in the hero of the story or tell when the characters are having fun.

As the story builds, so does the music. You can feel the tension just by listening. The hero is about to fall off a cliff into icy waters, or the sports team is down by one point with less than a second on the shot clock, or our favorite gang of talking toys is sliding into a furnace to their death... there is desperation in the air. The music is mounting, you are leaning forward, hiding your face, or bracing yourself for what might come next. The music has drawn you in, your emotions are getting involved, and...and...and...!

Suddenly, the hero finds his last bit of strength to climb back to safety, or the team's worst shooter finds the hoop and wins by one point, or the toys are scooped up from doom by their friends. The mood of the music turns, trumpets blare, strings might bring a tear of joy to your eye, and cymbals crash in celebration. "All is well!" it cries, and you take a deep breath, wipe the sweat off your forehead, and you can finally relax. The movie concludes, and everyone lives happily ever after.

If there was a soundtrack for Ephesians 2:1–10, it might help you connect with what Paul is trying to communicate, just as the movie soundtracks help with the stories I just described. Can you hear it? Read this passage and listen for the minor strings, brass, and cymbals:

> "*¹And you were dead in the trespasses and sins ²in which you once walked, following the course of this world, following the prince of the power of the air, the spirit that is now at work in the sons of disobedience—³among whom we all once lived in the passions of our flesh, carrying out the desires of the body and the mind, and were by nature children of wrath, like the rest of mankind. ⁴But God, being rich in mercy, because of the great love with which He loved us, ⁵even when we were dead in our trespasses, made us alive together with Christ—by grace you have been saved—⁶and raised us up with Him and seated us with Him in the heavenly places in Christ Jesus, ⁷so that in the coming ages He might show the immeasurable riches of His grace in kindness toward us in Christ Jesus. ⁸For by grace you have been saved through faith. And this is not your own doing; it is the gift of God, ⁹not a result of works, so that no one may boast. ¹⁰For we are His workmanship, created in Christ Jesus for good works, which God prepared beforehand, that we should walk in them.*" Ephesians 2:1–10

Did you hear it? Did the music change and turn from gloomy or frightening to cheerful or lighthearted?

There is a tension building in Paul's letter that we explored in the last chapter. The first three verses of Ephesians 2 are frustrating, sad, and debilitating. Death—spiritual death—is the problem; it is one that you cannot get rid of or out of. Paul uses the phrases "trespasses and sins," "sons of disobedience," "passions of flesh," and "children of wrath" to describe the reality of death and the impossibility of the problem ever being resolved. Those first three verses leave you with a distressing understanding of your desperately hopeless situation. There is no way out.

Until the first two words of verse four.

Two words that will change your life.

Notice how Paul begins the next section? Take your pencil and put a rectangle around the first two words of verse four.

"But God."

Can you hear all the people in the church at Ephesus breathing a sigh of relief as the reader gets to these two words?

Just those two words, "But God," can give you the security and peace you need to keep going. To know that whatever just happened is contrasted with God is enough to rest easy.

Think about it. Paul just described the condition that is common to everyone in the human race. Spiritual death. Dark. Scary. Irrevocable. And it leaves you helpless and hopeless.

But God.

Can you feel the tension dissipate from your heart and mind? The darkness has scattered. The fear has dissolved. The heavy fog has lifted from your heart, and you can see clear daylight

ahead. Somehow, it does not really matter what is in that daylight. Just the sight of it is beautiful.

Take a few minutes to reflect on those words "But God."

Write some thoughts about what God's presence means for you here.

If "But God" was not enough, the passage goes on to enumerate how that "But God" plays out. Take a look:

> "*¹And you were dead in the trespasses and sins ²in which you once walked, following the course of this world, following the prince of the power of the air, the spirit that is now at work in the sons of disobedience—³among whom we all once lived in the passions of our flesh, carrying out the desires of the body and the mind, and were by nature children of wrath, like the rest of mankind. ⁴But God, being rich in mercy, because of the great love with which He loved us, ⁵even when we were dead in our trespasses, made us alive together with Christ—by grace you have been saved—⁶and raised us up with Him and seated us with Him in the heavenly places in Christ Jesus, ⁷so that in the coming ages He might show the immeasurable riches of His grace in kindness toward us in Christ Jesus. ⁸For by grace you have been saved through faith. And this is not your own doing; it is the gift of God, ⁹not a result of works, so that no one may boast. ¹⁰For we are His workmanship, created in Christ Jesus for good works, which God prepared beforehand, that we should walk in them.*" Ephesians 2:1–10

We have some more marking to do. Ready?

Read through the passage again.

Underline that first participle phrase after "But God."
(A participle phrase describes the noun it is talking about.)
It tells us a little about God. It is only four words long.
Underline it in the text.

Paul describes God as being *rich* in mercy.

Rich. That word certainly has different meanings, and most of them have something to do with money. But make no mistake, Paul is not talking about money. He is talking about mercy. Considering the condition in which we find ourselves in Ephesians 2:1–3, we need mercy. We need the abundance He offers. He is RICH, and there is plenty for everyone. He will never come up short or just get by. He is RICH in mercy!

Mercy. This is the choice to withhold punishment from someone who has done something wrong and deserves to be punished but is not. Mercy says, "Yes, I know you deserve wrath, but I choose not to give it to you." Think of it in legal terms. Imagine you are standing before a judge for some law you have broken. Suppose it was a horrible crime, from which no one should be let go. After seeing all the evidence, hearing from the witnesses, and making a decision, the judge says to you, "You have been found guilty on all counts charged against you. You are punishable in every state and by every means. However, I have chosen to withhold your punishment. You are free to go."

The criminal here in Ephesians 2 is you, standing before the Judge, God. He says, "You are guilty, but I will show my mercy. You are free to go."

God is rich in mercy! The depth of your sin is no problem for His mercy.

For the Love of God

Before we can talk any more about mercy, we have to go on to look at the next phrase:

> *"...because of the great love with which He loved us..."*

This phrase is crucial to the passage, as any teacher of language would tell you. It contains the word "because." The word because shows a reason or source for the surrounding information. The entire passage is centered on the words that come after because.

> *"...because of the great love with which He loved us..."*

It is the love of God that makes the rest of the passage possible. Look again at verse 4 and following:

> *"⁴But God, being rich in mercy, because of the great love with which he loved us, ⁵even when we were dead in our trespasses, made us alive together with Christ—by grace you have been saved—⁶and raised us up with him and seated us with him in the heavenly places in Christ Jesus, ⁷so that in the coming ages he might show the immeasurable riches of his grace in kindness toward us in Christ Jesus. ⁸For by grace you have been saved through faith. And this is not your own doing; it is the gift of God, ⁹not a result of works, so that no one may boast. ¹⁰For we are his workmanship, created in Christ Jesus for good works, which God prepared beforehand, that we should walk in them."* Ephesians 2:4–10

Let's talk about this love Paul writes about. First, we must establish what kind of love Paul is referring to. In our culture, the word "love" is used for just about anything. We "love" chocolate, shoes, pizza, the color purple, Vera Bradley bags, and coffee. Is it the same love with which we love our moms, children, spouses, or best friends? I hope not! There is a difference between my love for chocolate and my love for my mom. In our language, the idea of "love" is very broad. Perhaps too broad. In chapter two, I mentioned the fact that in the Greek culture, there were three concepts of love: *eros*, *phileo*, and *agape*. These concepts are distinct and are more defined than our broad subject. *Eros* is romantic love; *phileo* carries the idea of familial or brotherly love (think "Philadelphia," the city of brotherly love); and the third, *agape*, is good will, benevolent, affectionate love. Which one do you think Paul is talking about here?

The depth of your sin is no problem for His mercy.

You got it. *Agape*. Benevolence. Kindness. Goodwill. Charity. This love always acts with the recipient's good as its motivation.

The Scriptures beg us to stop and consider, dwell on, and ponder the great love of God.

First John talks about this love of God:

> *"See what kind of love the Father has given to us…"*
> 1 John 3:1

One translation even uses the word *lavish* instead of given. We do not use that word much in our everyday speech but it is a marvelous word!

Lavish. To lavish something upon someone is to give generously, bountifully, extravagantly. It is a pouring out. God lavishes, pours out His love in a constant flow. He does not use a small dropper to ration out His love, or cover you with love like you baste the Thanksgiving turkey. He does not use a pitcher. A bucket is too small. Even a barrel is too limiting! God lavishes His love! He uses barrel, upon barrel, upon barrel, upon barrel. It is lavished, poured and poured and poured on us!

Overflowing. It never, ever ends. I am not talking about a cup of coffee that overflows a bit or even the bathtub water that you left running and is now making its way down the hall. I am talking about Niagara Falls! Have you ever been to the falls in person? I remember being awestruck the first time I stood next to the crest line. The famous Horseshoe Falls are 180 feet high and allow roughly 45,000,000 gallons of water over the crest line every minute during peak daytime tourist hours (that is about a million bathtubs full of water every minute),[6] and it does not stop when the tourists have gone home.

You cannot separate God from His love.

This incredible love is not just something that God does; it is who God is. He cannot help but give His abundant love, because He is love! You cannot separate God from His love. It is impossible. Love is who He is, not just something He does. Because it is His character, you can never lose His love. You cannot earn it or even walk away from it. You are loved by God. Nothing can hold back His overflowing love.

"...God is love." 1 John 4:8

But back up for a minute to the last chapter. Remember all that talk of spiritual death? Remember how your condition leaves you? Dead. Hopelessly, helplessly dead. Paul reminds us of this in the very next phrase, "even when we were dead in our trespasses…"

But God shows His mercy, His compassionate pity on you. Let me help you truly grasp this with a little imagery. Mercy is not just looking on someone and feeling sorry. This word

---

[6] http://www.niagarafalls.ca/living/about-niagara-falls/facts.aspx

implies a deep emotional response, one of true pity on an undeserving subject. What God does for the spiritually dead is the equivalent of seeing mangled road-kill on the side of the highway, picking it up, holding it close, and taking it home to nurse it back to health. You were dead, deformed, ugly. But He, rich, so rich in mercy, with His forgiving kindness, takes this compassionate pity and sees this ugly, dirty, filthy nothing, scoops it up, brings it into Him and says, "Aw, baby, I gotcha. I love you!"

Oh, what a love!

Take a moment and let that sink in. God reached down into your reality of sin, into your desperate situation and for no reason but His love, showed you mercy. You are loved. You may not always feel loved, but the truth of Ephesians 2:4 gives you the confidence to know you are.

Think about that for a moment. Pause here and write a prayer of thanks to Him for His love for you.

The Night I Found God's Love

I remember when I realized the depth of my sin and the extent of God's love for me for the first time. It was a Sunday night at church. (I have heard some say they were in church every time the doors were open. I think my dad opened the doors.) My parents were leaders in the church, involved in everything imaginable. Needless to say, I heard about God and Jesus even as a baby. I had heard about being saved from sins, but I did not really understand my personal need for that salvation until one Sunday night.

I do not remember a lot from my childhood, and honestly, I do not know the date or how old I was. But I do remember there was a special singing group for the service that night. I do not know who they were or where they were from, but I remember listening to them explain salvation. They said Jesus came to this earth to save me from my sin, and that I needed to ask for His forgiveness and accept that gift. God's Spirit impressed on me my personal need for God's gift. It was not enough to be in a Christian family, or go to church, or anything else I could manage in my elementary-aged mind (I think I was about 7 or 8). I knew I needed Jesus. As they told all of us there how we could be saved, I asked God to forgive me and to save me. I remember knowing for sure when I had finished praying that something was different. I remember having a sense that the decision I had made was real.

I was saved early in life. By God's grace alone, I have remained faithful for over forty years. There has been no wandering from God, no drugs, no alcohol, no addictions, none of the stuff that we would normally consider a part of a "good" testimony. For some time that really bothered me. I thought of my story as being lesser when compared to those who had been saved from their "lives of sin." But when I studied this passage in Ephesians 2, God helped me understand that it took just as much mercy and grace to save me as it did to save anyone else because I was dead. Helplessly, hopelessly dead. Having a past that includes "major" sin did not make it harder for God nor does it make someone more saved than me. God extended His grace to those who were dead, and that included me. I was born with a sin problem and needed rescuing. Now, I look at the strength of God's grace to keep me from further sin as a major triumph.

Not Your Average Love

His love starts all the action; the rest of the passage is a result of God lavishing His love upon us. Take a look at what happens in the rest of the passage.

> *"⁴But God, being rich in mercy, because of the great love with which He loved us, ⁵even when we*

were dead in our trespasses, made us alive together with Christ—by grace you have been saved—6and raised us up with Him and seated us with Him in the heavenly places in Christ Jesus, 7so that in the coming ages He might show the immeasurable riches of His grace in kindness toward us in Christ Jesus. 8For by grace you have been saved through faith. And this is not your own doing; it is the gift of God, 9not a result of works, so that no one may boast. 10For we are His workmanship, created in Christ Jesus for good works, which God prepared beforehand, that we should walk in them." Ephesians 2:4–10

Circle all the verbs (actions) that God does in verses 4–10 and list them here:

The first thing He does is makes you alive. He causes you to live after you have been dead. It is usually the other way around, isn't it? Living comes first, and then death. God, in His love and through His mercy, reverses the natural process and brings life after death instead of death after life. It is a specific, particular, very intentional action God chooses to do.

It really is more about God than it is anyone else. Take a look and see if you can find how many times Jesus Christ is referenced in the passage.

Six times Jesus Christ is mentioned (four times He is specifically named) as being intimately involved in these actions. Deity, whether it be Christ or God, is named or referenced a total of thirteen times in verses 4–10 alone! This passage absolutely centers on God, not us. The beautiful thing is that even though the passage centers on God and His love, we are the objects of it. We glean all the intended good from this passage. We are the beneficiaries of this passage. But the subject, and the very clear author, mastermind, and initiator of the actions in this passage is God.

If compassionate mercy and great love is not enough to excite you about what God does for you, keep reading. God's grace is introduced as a vital part of the work God does. Grace is mentioned three times throughout the passage, and it goes hand-in-hand with mercy. While mercy is withholding deserved punishment, grace is bestowing undeserved blessing. Not only has God rescued us from the punishment of sin (spiritual death), but He has blessed us with life!

> *"...by grace you have been saved..."* Ephesians 2:5

God, in His great love, and through His great mercy, has saved you by His great grace! Paul does not just brush over this grace thing. He mentions it again in verses 7 and 8. In fact, in verse 8, He even uses the same exact phrase as in verse 5.

> *"⁸For by grace you have been saved through faith. And this is not your own doing; it is the gift of God, ⁹not a result of works, so that no one may boast."* Ephesians 2:8–9

Here Paul explains the gospel without wasting or mincing words. God's grace is extended to you so that you can be saved, and you accept it through faith. But it is not because of anything you can do. It is a gift from God, by His grace. That is the beauty of grace. Grace, by definition, is undeserved; if you earned salvation with good works, it would no longer be grace.

It is like this: if someone was to outright give you a house, saying, "This is a gift. It is already paid for, I just want you to have it," you would pack up all your belongings, rent the moving truck, get some friends to help, and settle in to the new place—paint, clean, unpack, arrange the furniture, etc. After you unpacked, you would not go to the bank and ask about getting a mortgage for your new home. That would be a bit absurd, don't you think? The banker would explain there is no need for the mortgage; the house is already paid for, it is already all yours. This is what you are doing when you try to earn God's grace. Your salvation is already paid for—it is wholly yours. You cannot give it more value, or earn God's grace by doing good to others or giving to those who are needy. There is nothing to pay for. It has already been done.

So you may be thinking, how exactly does this salvation work? What really happens so that I am saved from death?

Good question! The answer is Jesus Christ!

Contrary to popular belief, Jesus Christ is NOT just a "Sunday School answer," He is THE ANSWER! Jesus Christ is your salvation.

Spiritual death is the punishment for sin, the consequence for sin. But, because God loved us with His great love, He provided a way to rescue you from that consequence. That way is Jesus Christ.

Jesus Christ is God, but He came in human form so that He might take on the punishment for the entire world and satisfy God's righteous wrath against sin. Because He was God, He was sinless, and therefore He was the only one who could pay the price for sin.

So He came as one of us, lived as one of us, and died as one of us, for the sin of the entire world. He died for every sin that has ever happened, that is currently happening right now, and for every sin that will happen in the future. He took the punishment for sin by dying on a Roman cross: a bloody, gruesome, horrific death. And He experienced the separation from God.

> *"But He was wounded for our transgressions; He was crushed for our iniquities; upon Him was the chastisement that brought us peace, and with His stripes we are healed."* Isaiah 53:5

> *"But God shows His love for us in that while we were still sinners, Christ died for us."* Romans 5:8

But the story does not end there. After three days in the tomb, Jesus Christ rose from the dead. God's power lifted Him from the depths of the grave and just like that, death was conquered. Now, because of His death and resurrection, life is available to all those who believe. His payment was enough to satisfy God's wrath, God's penalty for sin.

Have you made the turn from sin to believing that Jesus Christ is your only hope? That is all God requires for your salvation: your repentance—turning from your deadness, realizing that you cannot be perfect, you cannot gain Heaven, you cannot be alive by doing this yourself. Understand the reality of sin and turn from it. Believe that nothing else can bring you life. Not your good deeds, not your money, not your baptism. Only Jesus Christ.

> *"...Believe in the Lord Jesus, and you will be saved..."* Acts 16:31

> *"For God so loved the world, that He gave His only Son, that whoever believes in Him should not perish but have eternal life."* John 3:16

"But to all who did receive Him, who believed in His name, He gave the right to become children of God." John 1:12

"⁹Because if you confess with your mouth that Jesus is Lord and believe in your heart that God raised Him from the dead, you will be saved. ¹⁰For with the heart one believes and is justified, and with the mouth one confesses and is saved. ¹¹For the Scripture says, 'Everyone who believes in Him will not be put to shame.'" Romans 10:9–11

Put this all together. Because of God's amazing love, He worked through His kind mercy, and by His generous grace He presents this gift of salvation. He rescues you from spiritual death and provides life! All you have to do is accept it. By believing in the work of Jesus Christ, you accept the gift of salvation Ephesians 2 is all about.

There is no other way but Jesus.

Do you believe? If you have never made the decision to turn from your sin and accept God's gift of salvation, what is stopping you? God may not give you another opportunity, and without having a relationship with Jesus, you will spend eternity in Hell. God's love has made a way, only one way, to have a right relationship with God. There is no other way but Jesus.

Perhaps you have accepted God's gift of salvation. You know you will be in heaven. You have responded to the gospel. If that is true of you, take a moment to process the depth of what we have been talking about here. This should never evoke an "oh yeah, I know that already" response in you. You will never outgrow your need for the gospel.

So, if you are saved, do not rush past the basics of the gospel. Come back to them and with a humble heart of praise, thank God for rescuing you and pouring out His grace on you. THEN, take the next step of following Him and submitting to what He has for you.

Personal Reflection

Take some time to reflect on Christ's work of salvation for you. If you have already accepted God's gift of salvation, write a note of thanks to God. If you have not, write your thoughts, doubts, or questions here.

Chapter 4

A Look at the Big Picture

Do you remember watching or reading cartoons as a kid? My all-time favorite cartoon strip is the beloved gang of the Peanuts characters. Charlie Brown, Lucy, Snoopy…I love them all! One of the best things about cartoons is that you always know what the characters are thinking. Often, there are thought bubbles over the characters to show exactly what is going on inside their heads.

Sometimes I wish there were thought bubbles in real life, so I know what other people are thinking when I am teaching or speaking to them. I often wonder if they understand anything I am saying, or maybe they think it is completely dumb because they already know what I am telling them. Reading listeners' faces can be quite difficult at times. If you have ever taught any kind of class, you know what I am talking about.

Since this is a book, it is even harder to read your face or mind to know whether or not I am coming across clearly. So I am going to have to cover my bases!

Maybe you have a huge question mark hanging over your head in your thought bubble. You might be thinking, "But why? I do not get it. Why would God do that?"

Or maybe in your thought bubble the words, "So what?" can be found. You may be thinking, "I get what you are saying, and I have heard it all before. What really is the point?"

Those are valid questions, and ones I aim to answer in this chapter. They actually have the same answers, which makes it a little easier for both of us. So, let's dive in!

A Method to the Magnificence

Salvation is very purposeful. God has planned and carefully designed it with specific goals. It is not just some random thing that God decided to do because He was bored. He has grand purposes for sending Jesus Christ.

As we continue in Ephesians 2, we discover why God chooses to love us, and give us Jesus Christ. It is found in verse 7.

> *"¹And you were dead in the trespasses and sins ²in which you once walked, following the course of this world, following the prince of the power of the air, the spirit that is now at work in the sons of disobedience—³among whom we all once lived in the passions of our flesh, carrying out the desires of the body and the mind, and were by nature children of wrath, like the rest of mankind. ⁴But God, being rich in mercy, because of the great love with which He loved us, ⁵even when we were dead in our trespasses, made us alive together with Christ—by grace you have been saved—⁶and raised us up with Him and seated us with Him in the heavenly places in Christ Jesus, ⁷so that in the coming ages He might show the immeasurable riches of His grace in kindness toward us in Christ Jesus. ⁸For by grace you have been saved through faith. And this is not your own doing; it is the gift of God, ⁹not a result of works, so that no one may boast. ¹⁰For we are His workmanship, created in Christ Jesus for good works, which God prepared beforehand, that we should walk in them."* Ephesians 2:1–10

This is a look at the big picture. When you are working on a puzzle, it is always easier if you have the front of the box. The picture on the front of the box gives you the big-picture view—what it is supposed to look like when all of the pieces are together. That is what Paul does for us in verse 7; it is the front of the box. He gives us the big-picture view of God's plan. What is God's purpose in all of this? To show us His grace.

> *He desires that you see Him and His grace.*

We talked about both mercy and grace in the last chapter, and while they are very similar, they are not the same. God's mercy is His compassionate pity, withholding punishment, so you do not receive what you deserve. God's grace is Him giving you blessing you do not deserve.

Get this: He saved you by His grace so you would know His grace. One of the reasons God saves you is so that you will learn of Him. He desires that you see Him and His grace. There is a depth and richness to this grace that goes beyond its saving quality. This is very similar to the end of Ephesians 1. Paul prays for the Ephesians that they might understand His greatness, His distinction, and His eminence. That is what God wants for you as well.

> *"[18]...that you may know...[19]what is the immeasurable greatness of His power toward us who believe, according to the working of His great might [20]that He worked in Christ when He raised Him from the dead and seated Him at His right hand in the heavenly places..."* Ephesians 1:18–20

But this is a ceaseless learning of His grace. In Ephesians 2, Paul writes, "...so that in the coming ages..." God longs for you to continually learn and know His grace. It is so deep and so rich that learning about it has to be an ongoing thing! It is not one of these read-this-book-and-take-this-quiz things that you did in school. It is a subject that you continue to learn about, and God continues to teach you.

In Ephesians 2, Paul highlights God's greatness. We have seen that His great love is lavished on you (barrel upon barrel upon barrel...). We have seen His unending supply of mercy, and now we look at His grace. Through His grace, He gives you blessings that you do not, cannot, and will never deserve.

Because of sin, you deserve death. You deserve the punishment that sin incurs: spiritual death, separation from God. You deserve to die and never be right with God. You deserve death in its darkest, ugliest, most dreadful sense. But God does not desire to give you death; Jesus took it for you. What He does give you is blessing. He gives His grace.

> His glory is a purpose of His marvelous salvation.

The Greek word for grace is *charis*.[7] It is defined as that which affords joy, pleasure, delight, sweetness, charm, loveliness. That is a long way from the condition of spiritual death! It is good will, loving-kindness, the favor of God.

Allow me to remind you that this favor is coming from the Creator, the Almighty God, and not your friend, or your mom, your boss, your pastor, or even the president. The Almighty God, Creator of the Universe, is giving grace to sinners. You were sinful, acting against God in every way. He chose to give grace to you, to make you a friend. Because of Jesus Christ, you can go from being spiritually dead to being fully alive in Christ.

---

[7] http://www.blueletterbible.org/lang/lexicon/lexicon.cfm?Strongs=G5485&t=KJV

That is His grace. God's grace has been extended to you and pours out blessing upon blessing upon blessing. God's grace. I cannot understand it, but He does it...because He is God.

Glory

A second purpose for God's salvation revolves more around Him than it does you, as the text explains. In verse 9, Paul points out that it is not because of us that we can have salvation.

> *"8For by grace you have been saved through faith. And this is not your own doing; it is the gift of God, 9not a result of works, so that no one may boast."*
> Ephesians 2:8–9

His glory is a purpose of His marvelous salvation. Salvation is given to so that He can be glorified, honored, exalted. You do not earn it by anything you could do on your own. No amount of good works can ever obtain salvation. Why? Look in verse 9—"so that no one may boast."

Salvation is God's doing. He is the one who gets the glory. He alone is worthy. This is something you cannot share credit for. By yourself, you are unable to gain access to a holy God. But He made it possible, and He alone is worthy to receive the glory from it.

As I write this chapter, we have just finished the Christmas season. I love celebrating the first coming of Jesus Christ with my family each year. The season always conjures up memories of mom's cooking, playing with my siblings, and opening that one unforgettable gift, all with the classic Christmas music playing in the background. While Christmas is much more than just family and gifts, allow me to use the idea of a Christmas gift to illustrate my point.

When we give each other gifts for Christmas, we put thought, time, and money into the gifts. Some gifts are very thoughtful and planned out perfectly, so that the receiver will appreciate it. When you get a gift that you absolutely love from someone, who gets the glory in the whole exchange? Yes, you get to enjoy the gift, but the one who gave it to you gets the glory for it. Why? Because it was the giver who thought of the gift, making sure to find something that you would like. This requires a love for you as the motivation for giving the gift. It was the giver who thought of the gift, who took the time to buy or make the gift, and to wrap the gift. It was the giver who did all the work! All you have to do is receive it. While you get all the benefits of it, the giver gets the credit—the glory—for it.

It is the same way with God and His salvation. It is His gift (see verse 8). He is the giver. He loves and knows you, and He knows your need. He took the time to plan from the very beginning how salvation would work. He made everything possible for it, and all you have to do is receive it. You get to enjoy salvation, but He gets the credit for thinking, planning, preparing, and giving. God gets the glory!

Glory is not just something God earns, like a paycheck. Glory is something God already has, because He is God. His holiness, His righteousness, His justice, His creativity, His power, His love and His character are all a part of His glory. He is glorious because of who He is.

From the pages of Scripture, we know the glory of God is an awesome yet terrifying thing to behold. There are only a few instances recorded in Scripture of God showing His glory to humans.

Moses was one of the first humans to see the glory of God. We read in Exodus 33 that although Moses desired and asked to see the full glory of God, he was only allowed to see God's back, because seeing the glory of God's face would kill him.

Did you catch that? It would kill him. God's full glory is too much for a human to handle. No one is able to see all of His glory and live to tell about it.

> *"²¹And the LORD said, "Behold, there is a place by me where you shall stand on the rock, ²²and while my glory passes by I will put you in a cleft of the rock, and I will cover you with my hand until I have passed by. ²³Then I will take away my hand, and you shall see my back, but my face shall not be seen."*
> Exodus 33:21–23

In Exodus 34, it says that Moses' face shone brightly because he had been talking with God. Think about that. God is so truly awesome and powerful that just by talking to Him, Moses' face glowed. It says it shone so brightly that he had to put a veil over his face!

> *"²⁹...Moses did not know that the skin of his face shone because he had been talking with God. ³⁰Aaron and all the people of Israel saw Moses, and behold, the skin of his face shone, and they were afraid to come near him...³³and when Moses had finished speaking with them, he put a veil over his face."* Exodus 34:29–30, 33

Can you imagine talking to one so extraordinary, so powerful, and so glorious, that you had to walk around with your face covered because it was glowing so brightly? Incredible.

The brilliance of God's glory was also seen by others in Scripture. The New Testament disciples, Peter, John, and James, were shown the magnificent glory of Jesus Christ. In Luke 9, it says that Jesus' appearance changed and His clothes began to shine.

> *"29And as He was praying, the appearance of His
> face was altered, and His clothing became dazzling
> white...32Now Peter and those who were with him
> were heavy with sleep, but when they became fully
> awake they saw His glory..."* Luke 9:29, 32

The word translated dazzling here is described as being much like lightning: "To flash out like lightning, to shine, be radiant."[8] The glory of Jesus Christ is as bright and breathtaking as the phenomenons of the weather, and even much more.

The revealing of God's glory does not end there. In the book of Revelation, we are told of future events. The glory of God will dwell on earth for everyone to see. Jesus Christ will reign on earth as King of kings and Lord of lords, and His glory will be displayed in a very visible, awesome way.

> *"11Then I saw heaven opened, and behold, a white
> horse! The One sitting on it is called Faithful and
> True, and in righteousness He judges and makes
> war...16On His robe and on His thigh He has a name
> written, King of kings and Lord of lords."* Revelation
> 19:11, 16

God is a glorious being. He is an awesome God. He deserves every drop of glory the gift of salvation brings Him. He is not a ruler that needs an ego boost; He most certainly is worthy of all glory. When we try to earn our salvation by doing good works, we are actually stealing glory from Him. The glory rightfully belongs to Him; we have absolutely no entitlements to any of His glory.

The glory of God, in all of its grandeur and brilliance, is a purpose of salvation. The beautiful relationship of these purposes for salvation—His grace and His glory—allows you

---

[8] http://www.blueletterbible.org/lang/lexicon/lexicon.cfm?Strongs=G1823&t=KJV

to gain all the benefits from salvation, while God receives the deserved glory.

Good Works—Not For Salvation, But Because of It

There is a final purpose for our salvation, and it is found at the end of the passage. Verse ten sums up this entire section:

> *"For we are His workmanship, created in Christ Jesus*
> *for good works, which God prepared beforehand,*
> *that we should walk in them."* Ephesians 2:10

You are His work, to do His plan in His time. God designed you, created you, carefully put you together in Christ Jesus, and you are called His workmanship. Another translation uses the word *masterpiece* (NLT), and yet another uses the word *handiwork* (NIV). You are a product of His creativity, and He delights in you like a master craftsman would take pride in His most detailed, most breathtaking masterpiece. God feels the same way about you as perhaps Michelangelo did when he finished painting the ceiling of the Sistine Chapel. The Creator swells with pride as He steps back and presents His intricately designed masterpiece: you.

> *The Creator swells with pride as He steps back and presents His intricately designed masterpiece: YOU.*

But He did not stop there. First, He created you in Christ Jesus, and then He arranged things for you to do. Your purpose is good works. He created you, His workmanship, His masterpiece, for good works. The things He has planned for you to do fit magnificently with your strengths and talents. He created your works in light of how He created you.

He has it all laid out. There is no guessing, no dawdling, no impulsive decisions. God is not moving from day to day trying to figure out what to do with you. He does not make decisions on the spur of the moment. God is not up in Heaven saying, "Let's see, what should we do with (your name) today? Maybe we should...nah, not today. Or how about...No, I do not think so. Maybe I'll have her...yeah, that will work today."

That is not how it works. Instead, He has it all worked out for you.

Isn't it nice to know He has everything all figured out? It is already planned, and all laid out for you. Not only is He the Master Craftsman, He is also the Master Organizer! God has prepared and assembled things for you to do for Him.

The even better news is that God will give you the grace and the power to do those good works! He designed you and created you especially to do what He has planned for you. Just like the gift of His salvation gives Him glory, the good works also give Him glory when you do them through His grace—His plan, His way, His time.

That is amazing!

This is the bigger picture of God's beautiful plan of salvation. He did not think up this project on a whim. God has planned and prepared salvation for you with specific purposes to accomplish, and it comes full circle as we accept and implement it into our lives.

There is a hymn that speaks beautifully about the grace of God. It is one of my favorites. Read these words of Grace Greater than Our Sin[9] and ponder the deep, rich, extraordinary grace of God.

> Marvelous grace of our loving Lord,
> Grace that exceeds our sin and our guilt!
> Yonder on Calvary's mount outpoured,
> There where the blood of the Lamb was spilt.

---

[9] Lyrics: Julia H. Johnston. http://www.hymnsite.com/lyrics/umh365.sht

Chorus:
Grace, grace, God's grace,
Grace that will pardon and cleanse within;
Grace, grace, God's grace,
Grace that is greater than all our sin!

Sin and despair, like the sea waves cold,
threaten the soul with infinite loss;
Grace that is greater, yes, grace untold,
Points to the refuge, the mighty cross.

Dark is the stain that we cannot hide.
What can avail to wash it away?
Look! There is flowing a crimson tide,
Brighter than snow you may be today.

Marvelous, infinite, matchless grace,
Freely bestowed on all who believe!
You that are longing to see His face,
Will you this moment His grace receive?

Personal Reflection

Take some time now to recognize God's grace in your life. In what ways has God poured His grace on you? How has He blessed you with things you do not deserve? Be specific.

Thank God for these things. Write Him a prayer, or sing a song of thanks to Him to give Him the glory He deserves.

Give Him glory out loud! Talk to someone you know today and tell them about God's grace in your life.

What kind of "good works" has God prepared for you to do? List some things He has planned for you that you have done (or are doing) for His glory.

Describe how you are doing these things—are you fighting Him? Are your fists clenched? Or are you open-handed and grateful-hearted?

Now think of the things that perhaps you haven't done yet. Do you know of anything that God has prepared for you that you are not doing?

For the Love of God

Chapter 5

Love: No Flowers Needed

Last weekend I was given a grace-gift from God (a gift that God gives out of His grace). It was not a thing, like a package in the mail or a gift, but rather an experience. We had a get-together of some alumni basketball players I coached. They really do not need a reason to enjoy one another's company, but since this was a special weekend, many of them took time from their very busy lives and made the trip to campus with their families. They are a special group of women (and even some of their parents) who forged a special bond while at college and playing basketball. The bond is so tight, they refer to each other as "the family." Their presence was the grace-gift. We talked, laughed, talked, ate, talked…What a great time! Sometimes God gives special "packages" to remind us of His love and care for us.

There are smaller, more regular grace-gifts I have experienced recently. They do not always come in big experiences, but rather in the little day-to-day things, and they are often not as fun as a basketball alumni reunion. I realize many of these when I am driving. Perhaps you have never experienced this, but there are days when I think someone has written, "Cut this car off!" all over my car. Traffic lights see me coming and turn red. Road work, pedestrians, potholes, and traffic all seem to have secretly conversed and decided to give me "opportunities" to show God's grace in action. You see, left to myself, my reactions to those situations would be less than "grace-full." I get irritated at being delayed and sidetracked from my own agenda. It seems too easy some days to express my frustration verbally (I am very thankful for closed car windows!). But I do not have to have those responses. My life is no longer under the command of sin, but of God. When I choose to have a right response, rather than a natural reaction, I am enjoying a grace gift. His grace gives me the strength to respond correctly. When I allow God's Spirit to work His plan for my day—His timing of it, who will cross my path (and at what pace!), the playing out of my daily schedule—and submit my agenda to His plan for my life, I see the normal happenings with a different perspective. I see my need for God's grace and how abundantly He gives it.

Take the Grace of God and Run

Often I find myself—and perhaps you do, too—asking these questions of frustration: Why is this so hard? What is it that keeps me from walking as an object of His love? The answer is easy to find, but it is not easy to hear. The very same things that He has rescued you from are what keep you from God's plan. That list of "sins and trespasses" that we were found dead in have been relinquished as our dictators. You are not enslaved to

> You do not have to be haunted by your past any longer.

them as you once were; they are no longer your master. But they still seem to haunt you.

They haunt you every time you say or do something you know you should not. They haunt you every time you react to someone out of anger. They haunt you every time you act without thinking. Since all you have ever known is how to behave in the condition of spiritual deadness, you act as though you are still dead. You are no longer dead, but the "sins and trespasses" of your deadness still trouble you.

You walk inhibited. You walk as though you are dead; you believe you are inadequate, unable, without hope.

It is here you find another dimension of God's grace. His grace does not end with the gift of salvation. It does not end with just making you alive. It does not even end with good works for you to do. God's grace goes far enough to afford you the power to do those good works. By His grace, you are able to leave that which is behind—"sins and trespasses"—and do what is ahead—you were "created in Christ Jesus for good works."

God's grace gives you the power to do the good works for which you were specifically created. Before, when you were dead, you could not do anything. But when Christ makes you alive, He makes you healthy and productive. He has created you specifically for the good works He has planned for you. You are alive, and you have the ability to do good works.

You do not have to be haunted by your past any longer. Shed your shame, your feelings of inadequacy and hopelessness; they will not help you. His grace gives you the strength to take the next step, to do the right thing, to live full and free… to live knowing you are loved!

Do Not Believe Everything You Hear

Did you know that about one in ten men is color blind?![10] My family seems to have hit the jackpot on color blindness, because two of my three siblings are color blind. Both of them have trouble distinguishing between colors. This makes them very dependent on others when clothes shopping and can be a lot of fun for the ones helping! I remember one particular time we were all out shopping, and my brother

[10] http://www.ncbi.nlm.nih.gov/pubmedhealth/PMH0001997/

was looking for a pair of pants. We found a great deal on a pair of white pants, and on the way home, he asked the rest of us if we thought the pants were a good buy. I could not resist the opportunity and said, "Sure, I think they are really nice pants…if you like pink pants." My other siblings did not miss a beat. Together we had him believing he had just bought pink pants! He realized what we had done when he was trying to explain to my mom (who had no knowledge of what we had done) that he did not realize he had bought pink pants and that he really did not want pink pants. She said, "What are you talking about? They are not pink." At this point, my brother realized he had been conned. He had chosen to believe us, and it turned out to be bad advice. He trusted our "wisdom" and believed the wrong thing. In the end, he had indeed bought the right pair of pants but was listening to the wrong voice about that truth. He learned that day—do not believe everything you hear.

Newsflash! It is possible to make right choices! Through His grace, He gives you the ability to do so. But be careful who you listen to! The world around us says, "No, it is not possible to make right choices." We hear, "Follow your heart. It doesn't matter if it is right or wrong. Just follow your heart and everything will be ok." Burger King says, "Have it your way."[11] Nike says, "Just do it."[12] Debby Boone sings, "It can't be wrong when it feels so right" in her 1977 (I know, it is old) love song, *You Light Up My Life*.[13] Everywhere we turn, we are told it is too hard to do the right thing; it is easier to just do what you want at that moment!

But God says it is possible. His grace makes it possible in your life. He gives you the ability and the power to do the right thing; you have the great potential through His grace to

[11] http://www.thinkslogans.com
[12] http://www.cfar.com/Documents/nikecmp.pdf
[13] http://www.oldielyrics.com/lyrics/debby_boone/you_light_up_my_life.html

make good, upright, and pure decisions. It is possible; do not believe the lie that sinfulness is your only choice.

In fact, there are a lot of things the world yells at you that you should not believe. The world's "wisdom" is a lot of misinformation. In reality, it is just a skewed version of the truth of Scripture. The world's wisdom can be so close to what Scripture says, but yet so far from the heart of God. You are told by the world to accept everyone's beliefs and lifestyle. Scripture revolves around Jesus Christ as the only true way to God. You are encouraged to do good for special causes, but only if you get something out of it like fame, a tax deduction, or higher self-esteem. Scripture says that genuine love is the main ingredient in relationships and to care for others before your own needs. The world says that it does not matter what you do with your boyfriend as long as you love each other. Scripture begs us to honor God, not ourselves, with our bodies.

You must engage your mind in life.

And the list goes on. The world's wisdom sounds so good. Some of it is good, but not all of it is truth. You must compare what you hear to what Scripture says. You must engage your mind in life. Pay attention to what you hear and even to your own wandering thoughts. The Word of God must be the final authority; your mind must be sharp and discerning as you view what the world has to offer. Jesus said it like this:

> *"Behold, I am sending you out as sheep in the midst of wolves, so be wise as serpents and innocent as doves."* Matthew 10:16

Paul said it this way:

> "*15Look carefully then how your walk, not as unwise but as wise...17Therefore do not be foolish, but understand what the will of the Lord is.*" Ephesians 5:15, 17

You must understand there is a wide gap between the world's wisdom and the Word's wisdom. Do not believe the lies the world shouts at you. Know that through God's grace, you can make right choices. It is possible to know the right thing to do and then to actually do it. It is possible because of His grace. It can be hard at times—many times—but as Paul reminds us, "live self-controlled, upright, and godly lives in the present age" (Titus 2:12).

God certainly does not leave you hanging; He does not tell you to do good works without providing the means. He has created you especially for the good works He has planned for you to do. He has "wired" you just for them. Through His grace, you are guided and empowered to make right choices and successfully complete these good works.

However, you have responsibility, too. While God's grace gives you the power and ability to make right choices, sometimes you do not. Does that mean that God has forgotten about you or that He was not paying attention? No. God never overlooks anything, and nothing takes Him by surprise. He has supplied the grace to do good works, but it is our responsibility to use that grace and actually do the good works. You have to tap into the power God's grace provides and start living as though you believe you were created for great things.

There Is No Doubt
Let's take a final look (at least for this book) at Ephesians 2. Oh, what marvelous truth in these ten verses! Read through them again. Even read out loud if you would like! You have done a lot of specific marking in this passage throughout the

previous chapters. Reflect on what you have read and marked and allow the Holy Spirit to move in your heart and mind using the Scriptures. Take a few minutes to process what we have studied in Ephesians 2. Write down any thoughts. Underline, circle, or highlight as you feel led. What speaks to your heart from this small portion of God's Word?

> "[1]And you were dead in the trespasses and sins [2]in which you once walked, following the course of this world, following the prince of the power of the air, the spirit that is now at work in the sons of disobedience—[3]among whom we all once lived in the passions of our flesh, carrying out the desires of the body and the mind, and were by nature children of wrath, like the rest of mankind. [4]But God, being rich in mercy, because of the great love with which He loved us, [5]even when we were dead in our trespasses, made us alive together with Christ—by grace you have been saved—[6]and raised us up with Him and seated us with Him in the heavenly places in Christ Jesus, [7]so that in the coming ages He might show the immeasurable riches of His grace in kindness toward us in Christ Jesus. [8]For by grace you have been saved through faith. And this is not your own doing; it is the gift of God, [9]not a result of works, so that no one may boast. [10]For we are His workmanship, created in Christ Jesus for good works, which God prepared beforehand, that we should walk in them." Ephesians 2:1–10

I want you to see the drastic change that has taken place in just these ten verses of Ephesians 2. The passage begins with death. "But you were dead in your trespasses and sins..." There was nothing you were able to do that was of any merit by God's standards because you were dead inside. Spiritual death caused you to be an unprofitable creature. In fact, not only were you not doing anything profitable, you were doing destructive, sinful things. You were following sinful desires, walking in disobedience, immorality, and transgressions. You were unable to do anything of worth because you were completely and utterly dead. You sat helplessly in your condition, and you had no hope of finding your way out. It was impossible.

But as you move through the words of Scripture, you undergo a remarkable transformation. Jesus Christ comes and turns you from death and makes you alive. Because of His love and through His grace, you no longer have to be dead. You can escape the hold that sin has had on your life. You were dead, but He can make you alive.

Now, it is one thing to be alive; it is another thing to be productive. God takes you from a dead creature, makes you alive, and helps you become someone who is successful in doing great things for Him. What a transformation!

All of this is made possible by His love. You do not have to find a daisy for this one; you know you are covered in love. God pours His love on you barrel upon barrel upon barrel upon barrel. It never ends! Like Niagara Falls, its volume is unimaginable and its flow is continuous. His love is not something you have to keep guessing about or hoping for. It is always there, no matter what. There is no doubt in your mind or heart that you are loved extraordinarily, inexhaustibly, unconditionally, and eternally. You do not have to get up every day and wonder, "God loves me...God loves me not. He loves me...He loves me not..." There is no doubt: He loves me! No flowers needed.

Personal Reflection

So...Are you dead or alive? If you have never asked Jesus Christ to save you from your sin, and accepted His gift, then you are dead. But you can be alive, that is the good news!

If you have already been made alive by Christ through His salvation, how are you living? Are you walking in the truth that God is love and that His love is purposeful? Have you tapped into the power to do the good works God has planned for you?

Chapter 6

Free to Live!

But Wait, There is More!

What if I told you there was more to God's love than just the gospel? What if I told you that the gospel is just one part of God's big-picture plan for us? Would you want to know more?

Do not get me wrong: the gospel is huge. HUGE. Big enough that it should make us shout, "Oh what a love!" Have you declared that yet?

We have come a long way from where we started five chapters ago. We began at autopilot and spiritual death and then dove right into the marvelous ocean of God's love.

In Ephesians 2, we saw that His love is so massive that it takes a dead, filthy, ugly, good-for-nothing, sin-wrecked person and makes her alive and productive. Because of His great love, through His kind mercy, He gave His Son, Jesus Christ, in return for that sinner's (your) redemption. Jesus Christ took all the punishment you deserve and makes you alive. God did this so that you might know His grace. His grace is enough to transform that dead, filthy, ugly, good-for-nothing, and sin-wrecked person and make her into a beautiful, grace-knowing, good work-accomplishing masterpiece. The glory of it all goes to Him and Him alone, but you receive all the benefits of it. Oh, what a love!

We have established one thing: there is no doubt that God loves you. No doubt! His love has provided this amazing salvation. But here is the thing: too often you forget that you were in desperate need of that salvation. (Am I right? I know I forget it more than I would like to admit.) There was nothing you could do before Jesus Christ came to turn you from death to life. But you are forgetful. You stop living as though it means anything to you. "Yeah, yeah, Jesus saved me from my sin," you might say. It is not a flippant thing! Heaven and Hell are realities, but you forget and do not live like you believe it. You may very well believe it, but sometimes your life does not show it.

That is what Part Two of this book is all about. The love that God has shown—the immeasurable, amazing, incomprehensible, enormous, immense love—brings freedom! The Christian life is more than just an understanding of the gospel. God's love brings you freedom that you have never had before. In 1 Corinthians 9:23–27, Paul talks about that freedom, and that is where we are going to spend Part Two. I have included the passage right here for you:

> "*23I do it all for the sake of the gospel, that I may share with them in its blessings. 24Do you not know that in a race all the runners run, but only one receives the prize? So run that you may obtain it. 25Every athlete exercises self-control in all things. They do it to receive a perishable wreath, but we an imperishable. 26So I do not run aimlessly; I do not box as one beating the air. 27But I discipline my body and keep it under control, lest after preaching to others I myself should be disqualified.*" 1 Corinthians 9:23–27

From here, I want to show you four qualities that you can have because of that amazing love. We are going to build on God's love—Oh, what a love! But that is not all; I want to proclaim, "Oh, what a life!"

Because God loves you, you have a whole new meaning for life. The fact is that because of His love and through His grace, He has come and cleansed you, changed you, redeemed you, made you alive, and empowered you. Because of all that, you have freedom to live...Really live!

God did not create you just so you could fill up your day planner. Today's culture has us so busy doing everything that we cannot possibly live the way God intended for us to live. Our lives are so stacked, so full, that we are doing everything, but we are not passionate about anything. Passion is the first quality God's love supplies.

Because God loves you, you have a whole new meaning for life.

Our culture also has us believing that we do not have any purpose in life. You live, you die, and the world keeps turning. This is not true! God did not create you just so you could live on auto-pilot. You have purpose. You were created to do great things, just as Ephesians 2:10 clearly states. Purpose is the second quality God's love supplies.

A third quality you must have to really live as God intended for you to live is persistence. It is going to take some work, but because of God's love for you and the purpose He has given, you must be persistent at accomplishing what God has for you. He has promised the grace to do everything required of you.

Finally, the freedom you have for living includes pursuit. You were not created to run around in circles; you were created to run intentionally and for the goal: the prize. Your pursuit is connected with your purpose and it's driven by your passion.

The Games
To fully appreciate the weight of this passage, you have to make sense of when, where, and to whom the text was originally written. It is important to understand the historical setting. The context of the passage in 1 Corinthians 9 revolves around a particularly significant cultural event: The Isthmian Games.

Much like ancient Greek Olympic Games, the Isthmian Games were held every two years in honor of the Greek god Poseidon, god of the sea.[14] They began in 581 B.C. and took place near Corinth. Athletes competed in horse races, foot races, chariot races, wrestling, boxing, and music and poetry competitions.[15] These games were serious competition for serious competitors. There were strict rules regarding who was allowed to compete. These games were not for the "weekend athlete," or for someone who decided to participate on a whim.

Paul uses this idea of athletics throughout his letters because he knew his readers would understand. He was writing to people who were well acquainted with these ancient Greek games. It is possible some of them had even been to the games as spectators and seen first-hand the intensity of the competition. They had been a part of the atmosphere, had seen the intense competition, and appreciated the athletes' level of commitment. While the Isthmian Games are no longer held, you can understand the picture he is using. The modern-day Olympic Games carry the same intensity and excitement today. Every two years, the world watches as athletes compete in events they have been training for. Most

---

[14] Holman Bible Atlas p. 253
[15] Word Studies in the New Testament 3.235

of them have been working toward the opportunity their whole lives.

The paragraph of Scripture we will study in the coming pages revolves around athletics. I understand that you may not be an athlete; that is okay. It is actually not a problem at all. Paul is not using the example to motivate you to try out for a sport; he uses it as an illustration to communicate his point to his original readers and to you today.

Personally, this part of Paul's letter speaks powerfully to me. Athletics have been a big part of my life since I was a kid. We had a basketball hoop in our driveway that my parents wisely hung lower than the standard ten feet when I was young and then raised it as I got older. I enjoyed playing all kinds of games—from kickball in P.E. to keep-away on the playground during recess, whiffle-ball in the backyard, football, swimming, and biking—to name a few. I started playing competitive basketball as a sixth-grader and knew I had found a sport I could participate in for many years to come. I ended up playing through high school and college, and then went on to coach at the college level for twenty years. You could say athletics is a part of me. There is just something about it—the hard work, the success, the desire to get better at it, working with a team to accomplish a goal, spending extra time to improve as an individual—for me, there is nothing like it! Consequently, this portion of Scripture strikes a chord deep within me.

Like I said, no need to be worried here if you are not an athlete. It is really okay. You will still understand what Paul is saying. His example will still relate to you, and you will feel the strength of the Scriptures even if you have never shot a basketball in your life. So, relax. I am not going into a long discourse on the merit of athletics or suggesting a workout plan to get you started. It IS possible to be a godly woman if you are not athletic, or even interested in athletics at all. I simply want to show you how the idea of athletic training found in 1 Corinthians 9 can encourage you to really live as God has intended for you to live. It is safe for you to keep reading.

Now drop and give me twenty!

Just kidding! Keep reading.

In the remaining chapters, you will be shown the freedom you have to live—really live—in Christ. You will discover what it is like to live an intentional, uninhibited life because of the love—oh, what a love!—and grace God has provided. You will learn to live passionately, purposefully, and persistently, while you pursue God's best for your life. Fasten your seat belt, girl! When you close this book's cover, you will be shouting, "Oh, what a life!"

Personal Reflection

Knowing now what you do about God's amazing love, how do you think it should change the way you live?

In what ways do you desire your life to become more full—not in quantity but in quality?

Pray or write a prayer asking God to show you what He wants you to see as you continue in this book.

Chapter 7

Passionate, or Just Plain Crazy?

You are too busy.

I know I said this a few pages ago, but it bears repeating. You are too busy.

Our culture is full. Full of information, full of opportunity, full of people, full of…you name it. We find ourselves trying to do all of the options, trying to be all of the solutions, and if we are not, we think we are missing out. We are not really living. If we have the calendar full of activity, and every hour or every minute of every day holds something to do, someone to help, an errand to run, then we think we are living life the way it is supposed to be lived. If you are not getting the most out of your day, then you must not be doing enough for God, for others, or even yourself. Why do we believe this? Why do we keep spending our days as though busyness is all there is to life?

You are not called to busyness simply for the sake of being busy. While you indeed do a lot of things—a lot of good things—many times you do not do things based on your passions. You "do" because it is expected, and that is just the way life is. You do not really have a choice…do you? Yes, you do! Think about it: you are not called to a life of expectations. You are not called to a life of auto-pilot. You are called to a life of passion!

I think you know what I am talking about. You have seen passionate people before. Maybe you have noticed them among the spectators at a sporting event. I enjoy college basketball and, as I write, March Madness is right around the corner. On almost any given night, I can see thousands of fans packed in an arena to cheer on their team. Even if you do not like sports, you know the excitement I am referring to. The fans come ready to show their support. They carry signs, dress in their team's colors, paint themselves, put on wigs...and then there is the cheering! Sometimes in unison, other times random shouting, yelling—words, sounds, accompanied by jumping and clapping, waving of hands, foam fingers...I think you get the picture. All because they feel strongly about who should win that particular game. They love the game, its players, and this is how they participate.

Maybe you have even been one of these fans at one time or another, perhaps at one of your children's athletic events. Little League games have the unique ability to bring out the passion in parents across the country. Perhaps you have found yourself there, sitting in the stands, or, better yet, running along the sidelines cheering for your son or daughter. "Yeah! Go, honey! Good job! Keep running, you got it!" Sound familiar?

You are passionate about that, because it means a lot to you. It is clear to everyone watching you that you are excited about it, and that it is important to you—and it should be!

But how about life?

Now I am not saying you should bring your foam finger to church (sit on that mental picture for a moment), but do you have a passion for really living? Are you excited about having life the way God really intended it? Or are you living in expectations, auto-pilot, and busyness?

Before you close this book and think this is not for you, let's talk about the real meaning of "passion." Though it looks one way at a sporting event, that is not what it has to look like every moment of our lives. Just thinking about the energy that would require tires me out!

Passion Defined

Passion is a powerful emotion. It is intense enthusiasm for something. It is a keen interest in a particular subject or activity. It is fervor, excitement, zeal, delight. It is participating in your own life with a full heart.

Passion is not about going so hard that you eventually burn out. I would not want people to describe my life with the phrase, "Going, going, gone!" Passion should include an element of anticipation. It carries a desire to participate even if it is tiring or exhausting because it is accompanied with satisfaction in knowing what you have done was worthwhile. A passionate person who is tired and a burned out person may seem similar at first glance, but there is a difference. A burned out person is exhausted and seemingly mad at the world; she has nothing good to say about anything, because she is too tired to even think. She has exhausted herself with the "to-dos" trying to keep up with everyone and everything. A passionate person who is tired has the exhaustion that comes with satisfaction. Passion is the fuel that keeps an individual pursuing her goals because she believes there is purpose in what she is doing. But I am getting ahead of myself. Passion is not about expending energy but rather connecting with what is happening in and around you.

Passion IS about being you! It is not random; God has created you with distinct wiring, and when you are involved in doing something that fits you, you can do it with enthusiasm. There are things you naturally get excited about because they are a part of your life or are special to you. We might call those things what makes you "tick." These are the things that keep you going. God wants you to be who He has created you to be. Your expression of that may not be waving foam fingers as you stand in line at the grocery store, but it does include being actively engaged in what you are doing throughout the day. In real passion, you are free to be who you are. In fact, there is nothing more beautiful than being who He has created you to be! God wants you to be you. What freedom! So laugh, be serious, wave your arms (or a foam finger!) but live life as God designed it to be lived...as you.

Let's read 1 Corinthians 9:23–27 again. I want you to see the passion Paul uses as an illustration in the text to see how we can connect this to real life.

> "*23I do it all for the sake of the gospel, that I may share with them in its blessings. 24Do you not know that in a race all the runners run, but only one receives the prize? So run that you may obtain it. 25Every athlete exercises self-control in all things. They do it to receive a perishable wreath, but we an imperishable. 26So I do not run aimlessly; I do not box as one beating the air. 27But I discipline my body and keep it under control, lest after preaching to others I myself should be disqualified.*" 1 Corinthians 9:23–27

Take a moment to grasp what Paul is saying here. He is using the example of an athlete in training to make his point. A competitive athlete is passionate about one thing—winning. Her daily routine includes many expressions of that passion as she eats, works out, converses, etc. That is part of what Paul is referring to here. In this particular passage, he is talking about the Isthmian Games that I described in the last chapter. If you were an athlete training for the Isthmian Games, your workouts would have been guided by that one opportunity. Years of your life (for many, from childhood) would be spent working toward those games. It required your utmost attention, your highest determined effort, and focused energy.

Passion needs focus. Without it, all the hype is merely undirected energy. Craziness. If your passion does not have anywhere to go, a direction, it is likely to do more harm than good. An athlete cannot afford to waste energy—misdirected or harmful.

You cannot have blurred vision when it comes to life.

What is focus? A focus is what my mind is zeroed in on. It is what my life is centered on, what I think about. My center point. Having a focus is what enables me to see clearly.

If you wear glasses, you know exactly what I am talking about.

What if one day you got up in the morning and decided you did not need your glasses? You just decided not to put them on. You make your way through the house, feeling your way around, knocking things over. You brush your teeth with hair gel instead of toothpaste. You put the milk in the pantry and the cereal in the fridge. You cannot read the newspaper. You can't find the remote. Your car keys are around here somewhere.

Without your glasses, your eyesight lacks focus. Your world is blurry, your routine is hampered, you spend extra time doing things that should be easy, and in the end, you may accomplish very little. You may find yourself going every-which-way and end up doing damage instead of being productive.

You cannot have blurred vision when it comes to life. Often, you may go through life in a haze—you are doing things because of expectations, but you cannot see very well so you just keep going full-throttle because you think that is what life is all about. But it is not. Your passion, that ability to do things with a full heart, needs focus, to give you direction and enable you to be productive as you do the life God has called you to do. Living without focus can result in speeding through the days knocking things over and destroying more than you are building.

There is a focus in 1 Corinthians 9. Can you find it?

> *"²³I do it all for the sake of the gospel, that I may share with them in its blessings. ²⁴Do you not know that in a race all the runners run, but only one receives the prize? So run that you may obtain it. ²⁵Every athlete exercises self-control in all things. They do it to receive a perishable wreath, but we an imperishable. ²⁶So I do not run aimlessly; I do not box as one beating the air. ²⁷But I discipline my body and keep it under control, lest after preaching to others I myself should be disqualified."* 1 Corinthians 9:23–27

This passage revolves around the gospel. Paul claims the gospel as His focus: "I do it all for the sake of the gospel..." Everything that Paul does is for the gospel. To proclaim the gospel, to live the gospel, to love the gospel, to further the gospel. The gospel is his focus. All of the energy that his passion collects is focused on, or put toward, the gospel. The rest of the passage flows out of that focus.

Does your focus include the gospel?

What is your focus? Do you have one? What are you living for? What do you love to talk about? What defines you? What kind of glasses do you put on in the morning?

Maybe it is your family. Your husband. Your kids. Maybe it is your ministry, or your church. Perhaps it is your career, or your talents or a hobby. Maybe it is your relationships. Your best friend or friends. What is your focus? Those are all good things. But I want to go one step deeper. Why do you do what you do? Is it to fulfill expectations, to please someone, to gain acceptance? Is your focus God-centered or you-centered? Does your focus include the gospel? Our focus should be to please Jesus, the One who died for us, is praying for us, and has given us the Holy Spirit to empower us to do God's plan.

Paul urges his readers to grab hold of the gospel. Make it the center of your life. Set it as your focus. It does not change. It will never change. You can hold on to it forever. Just a few chapters later, Paul makes clear to us just how important the gospel is and what our focus should be:

> "*1Now I would remind you, brothers, of the gospel I preached to you, which you received, in which you stand, 2and by which you are being saved, if you hold fast to the word I preached to you—unless you believed in vain. 3For I delivered to you as of first importance, what I also received: that Christ died for our sins in accordance with the Scriptures, 4that He was buried, that He was raised on the third day in accordance with the Scriptures.*" 1 Corinthians 15:1–4

Paul is very clear about how he feels about the gospel. It is of "first importance." He wants his readers to understand and is encouraging them, "Bring it back. Get it straight! This is first. This is Truth with a capital T!" Jesus Christ loved us, died for us, and now lives, still loving us. The gospel! Do not lose sight of it. Do not let it out of your grasp. Keep the gospel as your focus, because when the gospel is your focus, all those other things I mentioned earlier will fall in line. You can decide to choose something else to be your focus, but sooner or later you will lose your other priorities. Sooner or later, you end up blurring everything in your life, and that is no life at all.

Living with the gospel in view helps you make right choices in the every day details of life. It helps in the big things, like spending money wisely, loving people when it is not easy, and doing the right thing even if it is not easy or popular. It reminds you that God's goal is always your good and His glory. Living with the gospel in view helps in the little things, too, like being thankful when all the traffic lights are timed against you, the person in front of you in line can't find her wallet, the eggs break on the way home, each of your kids needs you right now, the tub is leaking, the washing machine will not spin out, and the heat has not been on since yesterday afternoon. A gospel-focused life benefits every area of life.

Your focus is the what of passion. We need focus. We need the gospel.

A New Word
It seems that our culture of busyness is pushing one very important word out of our vocabulary: "no." We seem to use it less and less, and our lives take on more and more. It is time we learn it again.

Gaining focus is a good place to start. Having focus will help us say "no" to other priorities and say "yes" to the gospel.

Passion needs focus, but it also needs boundaries. Using that word can perhaps carry some negative connotations. Boundaries tell you where you cannot go, right? I suppose you could look at it that way. But perhaps it might help if we think of them as fences.

Fences not only tell you what you should do, or where you should be, but they also serve as directional assistants. They are not just barriers to keep you out; they also keep you on track. They keep your focus on the gospel. When you start to wander outside of your focus, they gently push you back onto the road. They remind you that there are indeed guidelines that God has put in place for you. They teach you to become proficient at saying "no" to things that you do not need.

Paul draws the parallel to the Isthmian Games:

> *"Everyone who competes in the games goes into strict training..."* 1 Corinthians 9:25a (NIV)

The athletes' training for the Games certainly had fences. Some they built for themselves and some were put there by the rules of the Games. For example, two fences were automatically built before one could even think about being a competitor in the Isthmian Games. Fence number one: you had to prove you were a Roman citizen. If you did not belong to Rome's empire, you were not eligible to compete. Fence number two: you had to prove that you had trained for the Games for at least a solid year. An entire year of physical training and conditioning was required to even sign up for it. This was no local 5-K where you could show up, pay the entry fee, run the route and get the t-shirt. Oh, no. This was serious business and they wanted to be sure the competitors were serious as well.

These athletes lived intentionally. They were careful about what they ate, where they went, and what they did. There was a right way to train for the Games, and there was a wrong way. Some of their training "fences" included what they would or would not do in their social lives. They lived within their parameters, their fences, so they could train profitably. They built fences for themselves so they could train well. They learned to say "no" to some things because it was not within their focus.

I enjoy participating in a lot of different activities, and there are so many options—church Bible studies and small groups, music ministry, Sunday school teaching, mentoring/discipling students, community events, renovations in my house, taking online classes, personal quiet times, coaching, speaking and the studying that goes with it…and somewhere in there I would like to spend time with friends. So many things to do. All of them were good, and honestly, I tried to do those things all at once. Do not ask me how—I have no idea. I can tell you, however, that doing all of them left me weary and passionless. One day, a friend looked me in the eye and said, "Sherrie, what are you going to drop? You cannot do it all." She was right, and as I look back, I really needed her to tell me that. I needed her to give me permission to stop going so hard. If that is you today, here's your permission: you do not need to do it all! What are you going to say "no" to? Your schedule may still be very full; some seasons in our lives require that. But saying "no" to things—perhaps even good things—and "yes" to things that are guided by your focus can actually fuel your passion.

One thing is for sure: your parameters must include saying "no" to sin. God has called you to live a righteous and godly life, and that means saying "no" to the things that do not help you toward that goal. It is NOT okay to do what you want just because it feels good or makes you "happy." Remember, the gospel is to be your focus. When that is true, you cannot continue saying "yes" to sin.

God's stated intention in saving you is to change you to look like His Son, Jesus. So, if your focus is the gospel, there should be some change in your life. Others should see Jesus lived out in you. What you say, how you treat others, what you do with your time and money…all should reflect God's values and His intentions for you. When they do not (notice I said "when" because we are human, and that happens), your boundaries send up flares because you have stepped away from what is central—Jesus—and put yourself in His position. When that happens, your passion drives you to your knees to cry out for forgiveness. Then you get up and do the next right thing.

Play the Moment

Passionate people live within their guidelines. They understand their role is not to do everything, to be everywhere, all the time. This is what distinguishes a passionate person from a just plain crazy one!

Busyness is not the answer. Do not get stuck thinking it is your job to be everything for everyone. I hate to break it to you, but girl, you are not "it!" I am not "it!" Our culture wants us to be, but that is not what passion and God's intended life for us includes.

> *Others should see Jesus lived out in you.*

Your life is not yours to do as you want; you have been created with intention and wired to enjoy what God has made you to do. How you live, think, and act should show your passion, but it should also show your focus. What you say "yes" to and the sin that you say "no" to should reflect what is most important in your life.

As a coach, I wanted my players to be focused. I did not want them to think about how many minutes they played, the number of people in the stands, or what their hair looked like. I did not want them to think about the last play or the next two plays. I wanted them to think about just one thing: that moment and what they needed to do right then. I used to tell them, "Play the moment." I hope it translated into real life for them…to live the moment. You do not have to do everything and be everywhere. Live within the guidelines

God has set. Stay inside the fences. Keep the gospel as your focus. Learn to say "no." Play the moment.

So, are you passionate? Or just plain crazy?

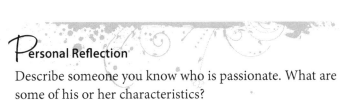

Personal Reflection

Describe someone you know who is passionate. What are some of his or her characteristics?

Describe yourself; how has God created you? Name three things that you do well.

What is your life's focus? (If you are not sure, ask a few friends that know you well for some input.)

What do you need to do to change your focus to the gospel?

Is there something in your life you need to say "no" to in order to become passionate? Is there extra activity in your schedule? Is there sin in your life that needs to be confessed and changed?

Chapter 8

You ARE On Purpose!

Quiz time! Can you match the award to the profession or event?

Oscar	Tour de France
Green Jacket	National Basketball Association
Yellow Jersey	NCAA Football
Stanley Cup	Olympics
Tony	Hollywood
Larry O'Brien Trophy	Music
Superbowl Ring	Theatre
Heisman Trophy	National Football League
Gold Medal	Writing
Grammy	Masters Golf Tournament (PGA)
Pulitzer Prize	National Hockey League

At the Masters Golf Tournament (PGA), it is a Green Jacket.[16] In the Tour de France, it is a yellow jersey.[17] In the National Hockey League, it is the Stanley Cup.[18] In the National Basketball Association, it is the Larry O'Brien Trophy.[19] In NCAA Football, it is the Heisman Trophy.[20] In the Olympics, it is a gold medal.[21]

---

[16] http://www.masters.com/en_US/index.html
[17] http://www.topendsports.com/events/tour-de-france/jerseys.htm
[18] http://www.nhl.com/ice/page.htm?id=25432
[19] http://www.mapsofworld.com/pages/trophies/basketball/larry-o-brien-trophy/
[20] http://www.heisman.com_
[21] http://www.olympic.org

These are all major sports awards. The award looks different from sport to sport, but in the end, every athlete is working for something.

It is not just athletics. There is a top prize in every profession. In Hollywood you have the Oscars for movies,[22] the Grammys for music,[23] and the Tonys for theatre.[24] For writers, it is the Pulitzer Prize.[25] In fact, there is an award or title for just about every line of work you can think of or imagine.

We could use another name for all of these awards.

Purpose.

That is right. Purpose. Everyone is working for something. Whether it is a trophy, a ring, a medallion, or a title, the award is ultimately what the competitor is working for.

An athlete's purpose is to win. Nobody shows up to the game or event and says, "Shoot, I hope I get second today!" No, of course not! All the conditioning, practices, scrimmages, and the mornings in the gym were not so you could bring home a nice shiny participation ribbon. Every athlete trains and steps out on the court, the field, the track, or the ice with one thing in mind: Win.

Look how Paul draws the parallel in our passage:

> *"[23]I do it all for the sake of the gospel, that I may share with them in its blessings. [24]Do you not know that in a race all the runners run, but only one receives the prize? So run that you may obtain it. [25]Every athlete exercises self-control in all things. They do it to receive a perishable wreath, but we an imperishable. [26]So I do not run aimlessly; I do not*

---

[22] http://www.oscars.org
[23] http://www.grammy.org/recording-academy
[24] http://www.tonyawards.com/en_US/index.html
[25] http://www.pulitzer.org

> *box as one beating the air. ²⁷But I discipline my body and keep it under control, lest after preaching to others I myself should be disqualified."* 1 Corinthians 9:23–27

Passion needs purpose to keep going. Purpose is what drives passion. Focus keeps the passion under control, but purpose gives passion its fuel.

Paul is using the example of competition. The prize is what drives the athlete. All of the competitors run, but there is only one prize and one winner. Run—compete, work—so that you are the one that gets the prize.

Paul is talking about motivation. Run so that you win. Run so that you cross the finish line having left everything you had on the track. After they have helped you up off the ground, they hand you a shiny trophy and suddenly everything you have worked and trained for has all been worth it. Run with purpose.

What are you running for? What are you living for?

You ARE on purpose!

Let me stop there for a minute. I want you to know, first of all, that you—yes, you—have a purpose. Let me repeat that. You have a purpose! You are not worthless!

Satan loves to whisper that lie to us. "You are worthless. Quit trying. Who do you think you are? Nobody cares about you! You are never going to be good enough." He is relentless when it comes to this lie. Do not believe it. Refuse to listen to it. It is a lie.

Pianist, singer, and songwriter David Meece[26] knows the pain of these words. His father was an alcoholic, and he admits that he does not remember much of anything good about

---

[26] Hear David's full testimony at http://www.davidmeece.com.

him. The words "You are worthless!" that were screamed to him by his father in a drunken rage haunted him for years. He believed the lie, even after he had written best-selling songs, toured as a concert pianist, and performed with symphony orchestras worldwide as a teenager. But David could not be convinced that he was any good at all. He had believed the lie and had become paralyzed by it. Until finally, he stopped listening to the lie, and he started listening to the truth.

Listen to the truth of God's love for you. Stop listening to Satan. Pay no attention to the lies he whispers to you. Listen to God! Know the truth of your life: you do have purpose! God says, "You are precious! You are valuable! You are cherished! I love you and have given you purpose for this life!"

A well-known west-coast author published a book that aims to bring people back from Satan's lies. In *The Purpose Driven Life*, Pastor Rick Warren uses the truth of Scripture to re-train readers' thinking patterns about their value. Chapter two is called "You are Not an Accident." In it, Warren says, "God never does anything accidentally, and He never makes mistakes. He has a reason for everything He creates. Every person was designed with a purpose in mind."[27]

Listen to the truth of God's love for you.

You are not an accident! You are completely on purpose. God made you intentionally and He loves you immensely. You were not a surprise to God nor are you a mistake. You are on purpose. Your life is significant, it does have meaning, and you do have worth and value in God's plan.

---

[27] Warren, Richard. *The Purpose-driven Life: What on earth am I here for?* Grand Rapids, MI: Zondervan, 2002. 23. Print.

Know the truth of your life. You are here because God wants you here. Let the words of Scripture resonate within you:

> *"[29]For those whom He foreknew He also predestined to be conformed to the image of His Son, in order that He might be the firstborn among many brothers. [30]And those whom He predestined He also called, and those whom He called He also justified, and those whom He justified He also glorified."* Romans 8:29–30

> *"...even as He chose us in Him before the foundation of the world, that we should be holy and blameless before Him..."* Ephesians 1:4

> *"For we are His workmanship, created in Christ Jesus for good works, which God prepared beforehand, that we should walk in them."* Ephesians 2:10

> *"[13]For You formed my inward parts; You knitted me together in my mother's womb. [14]I praise You, for I am fearfully and wonderfully made. Wonderful are Your works; my soul knows it very well. [15]My frame was not hidden from You, when I was being made in secret, intricately woven in the depths of the earth. [16]Your eyes saw my unformed substance; in Your book were written, every one of them, the days that were formed for me, when as yet there was none of them."* Psalm 139:13–16

Scripture is clear about God's love and delight in you. God designed and created you, with marvelous intricacies. The way you are wired is on purpose. God made you to be you! Do not forget it. Do not listen to anything but the truth. You are on purpose.

M.G.L.G.

Everyone has a purpose. No one flies under the radar here. You have a purpose—His purpose. The reason for your passion, the reason you are focused, the reason you run within your parameters is to glorify God. The "winning" is not to make yourself look good, like our culture encourages. The "winning" is to make Him and His grace in your life evident.

The best definition I have heard about glorifying God is in a book by theologian and author John Piper called *Don't Waste Your Life*. It is the best thing I have read on glorifying God. He talks about the fact that we are supposed to exalt, or magnify, Him. Piper writes,

> But when you magnify like a telescope, you make something unimaginably great look like what it really is. With the Hubble Space Telescope, pinprick galaxies in the sky are revealed for the billion-star giants that they are. Magnifying God like that is worship...God created us for this: to live our lives in a way that makes Him look more like the greatness and the beauty and the infinite worth that He really is.[28]

To glorify, or magnify God, is what we were made for. This is our purpose.

As a coach, this was something I wanted to be sure our players understood. When I talked to them about what it meant to "glorify God," I used the phrase "make God look good." We used the initials, "M.G.L.G." That is our goal—that is our purpose. Make God look good.

What exactly does that look like? Well, to an athlete it looks like working hard and using your strength and abilities for

---

[28] Piper, John. *Don't Waste Your Life*. Wheaton, IL: Crossway, 2003. 32. *Print.*

the good of your team and school. It is giving an all-out effort with excellence and a determined spirit. When you play with heart and use the abilities God has given you, He takes pleasure in it, and others see His character in your effort.

When I complain (in the athletic arena or in everyday life), I do not make God look good, capable, or loving. Think about it. When I complain about the weather and whine because it is too hot, or too cold, or wet or just not what I want, God does not look gracious, or great, or even aware of what is going on. When in fact, He is in total control, well aware of my needs—not to mention meeting all of them.

Even in the Old Testament we find the M.G.L.G. principle. Psalm 9 holds a prayer of David to the Lord for this very thing. David, a warrior, writes amid the battles of life. Even though he is experiencing oppression and times of trouble, he remembers the goodness, righteousness, and justice of God. In verses 13 and 14, David prays for the ability to fulfill His purpose of glorifying God:

> *"¹³Be gracious to me, O LORD! See my affliction from those who hate me, O You who lift me up from the gates of death, ¹⁴that I may recount all your praises, that in the gates of the daughter of Zion I may rejoice in Your salvation."* Psalm 9:13–14

David calls out to God, "Lord, please help me so that I can make You look good. Help me so that everyone can see that it is You, and only You. That is what is most important." God made you to glorify Him. He alone is worthy.

Piper further explains "glorifying God" in his book, *Don't Waste Your Life.* Perhaps you have heard it before. He states, "[God] is most glorified in us when we are most satisfied in Him."[29]

---

[29] Piper, John. *Don't Waste Your Life.* Wheaton, IL: Crossway, 2003. 36. Print.

Did you catch that? He is most glorified in us when we are most satisfied in Him. When we do what we are designed to do—and enjoy Him while doing so—God receives the most glory, is best magnified, and is fully exalted.

All of creation is doing what God designed it for: His glory. That is one of the things I love about living in the mountains of Pennsylvania. I love walking outside and seeing the beauty of the mountains, hearing the wind rustling through the trees. The Scriptures talk about creation proclaiming the glory of God:

> *"For His invisible attributes, namely, His eternal power and divine nature, have been clearly perceived, ever since the creation of the world, in the things that have been made..."* Romans 1:20

> *"The heavens declare the glory of God, and the sky above proclaims His handiwork."* Psalm 19:1

> *"...The mountains and the hills before you shall break forth into singing, and all the trees of the field shall clap their hands."* Isaiah 55:12

I love to leave my office and walk down the sidewalk of the beautiful college campus where I teach. The sidewalk that runs between the two major buildings and along the student dorms is lined with huge maple trees. In the summer and fall when the warm breeze blows through them you can hear the rustling leaves—they are clapping their hands. They are praising God, proclaiming His glory and handiwork. They are saying, "Yeah, God! Yeah, God!" And then the birds. They are singing the same song. "Yeah, God! God made me!" The

All of creation is doing what God designed it for: His glory.

flowers, the beauty of the mountains, the colors of the fall—all of creation is doing what it was designed to do.

That is what I want to do, too. I want to join creation and do the same thing. God has created me for a purpose, and I want to fulfill it. Glorify God. Magnify Him. Make God look good.

Worth It

Sometimes fulfilling your purpose is not as easy as clapping your hands when the wind blows. I gotta tell you, sometimes it is hard. Really hard. We live in a world of pain and heartache, but your purpose remains the same. Sometimes making God look good is easier said than done. Take, for example, the story in John 9.

In John 9, we meet a blind man. It says that he had been blind since birth. He had never seen anything, and there was nothing he could do about it. One day Jesus and His disciples were walking by this blind man, and the disciples wondered why the man was blind. The religion of the day assumed that if someone had such an ailment, it was because of sin. Listen to the conversation:

> "*2And His disciples asked Him, 'Rabbi, who sinned, this man or his parents, that he was born blind?' 3Jesus answered, 'It was not that this man sinned, or his parents, but that the works of God might be displayed in him.'*" John 9:2–3

The blind man had the same purpose we do: to glorify God, to make God look good. His blindness was not because of a certain sin that he or his parents had done. God was not punishing the man with blindness. He was blind so that he could bring glory to God. Watch what happens next:

> "*6Having said these things, He spat on the ground and made mud with the saliva. Then He anointed the man's eyes with the mud 7and said to him, 'Go,*

> *wash in the pool of Siloam' (which means sent). So*
> *he went and washed and came back seeing."* John
> 9:6–7

Jesus restored his eyesight, and the text does not say, but I'm sure the man was seeing with better than 20/20 vision. As you can imagine, he was overjoyed! He praised God because of it. His blindness became perfect sight and brought glory to God. He fulfilled his purpose, even though blindness was part of it. It may not have been easy, but the glory and fame that God received that day through this man's life was worth it. He made God look so good!

Sometimes, though, life does not always turn out "like it should." Sometimes your purpose to glorify God does not come with a nice little rainbow at the end. The Scriptures are full of people who did not have a great life but are honored as those who glorified God. Take, for example, Stephen. Stephen was one of the early church's first deacons. The disciples chose seven men to help them with specific tasks in the ministry of the early church. In Acts 6:5, it says that Stephen was "a man full of faith and of the Holy Spirit." He was chosen to work alongside the disciples because he was a man of God. He had been following the Lord and working for Him. We do not know much about Stephen, because he shows up in Acts chapter 6 but does not live past chapter 7.

Because of Stephen's character and wisdom, his enemies did not like him. They told lies about him, got a crowd riled up, and eventually got him arrested. Unfortunately, the ensuing trial did not turn out well for Stephen. He stood before the council of the religious leaders, spoke to them from the Scriptures, and then was dragged out of the city. There, he was stoned.

Stephen probably was not planning on spending his life that way. There he was, minding his own business, doing the work of God, ministering to people, and suddenly he's ridiculed, arrested, and stoned to death. Now I do not know about you, but that is not how I would consider life "turning out like it should." Surely, Stephen was excited to continue serving the Lord and probably anticipated a much longer life to do so.

But God's purpose was fulfilled in him, and He used Stephen for His glory. As an early martyr of the church, Stephen glorified God through his life—and his death—even if it did not "turn out like it should."

The Scriptures are littered with people whose lives did not pan out like they had planned. Joseph was bullied by his brothers, worked as a slave, and then landed in jail for a crime he did not commit. Moses left palace life to roam for forty years. Ruth lost her husband, brother-in-law, and father-in-law in the prime of her life. David lost a child as a result of his sin. Job was certainly left clueless when his life was stripped bare.

His glory is always worth it!

Jonah got to know a fish too well. John the Baptist lost his head—literally. Peter sat in prison more than once. Paul was shipwrecked. Nearly all of the disciples were martyred for following Jesus Christ.

Everywhere you look in the Scriptures, there is someone who was probably wondering what God was doing in their lives. God used each story to bring glory to Himself. The fact that we are still talking about them today is a witness to God's work!

Sometimes making God look good is easier said than done. In the midst of the pain, it can be very hard to see the big picture. But you must know that you still have a purpose, and God is going to use it to bring Himself glory. His glory is always worth it!

God's glory is worth the pain of the car accident that left your young husband paralyzed. It is worth the pain of your newborn baby's birth defect. It is worth the pain of your parents' divorce that sent you reeling as a college sophomore. It is worth the pain of betrayal from good friends. It is worth the pain of an empty bank account, a spouse's unfaithfulness, or your son's drug addiction.

These are things that may leave you wondering what in the world God is doing. They might even make you question following God altogether. These days may come, and they will bring heartache. But please know, you must know, that God is fulfilling His purpose in you. He is using you for His glory. Your life may not be "turning out like it should be," but do not let your ideas of what life "should be" limit you in God's work. He will use you, despite and perhaps even through the heartaches and circumstances of your life. You have purpose. God will use you!

Know Your Purpose
The ancient Greek philosopher Socrates is credited with the proverb, "know thyself."[30] The old adage encourages its hearer to study herself and understand how God made her. This is where you will find your purpose. Know thyself. Know how God has made you. Know your talents and your passions. This will lead you to your purpose, and make it evident to everyone watching you.

An athlete's purpose is very evident. It is implied. You step out there on the court and you are there for a reason: to

---

[30] http://www.neo-philosophy.com/Phil101Week5.html

compete. Paul, continuing with the athlete metaphor in 1 Corinthians 9, is saying that your purpose should be obvious. Make it apparent to everyone around you what you intend to do.

You may be familiar with the movie *Chariots of Fire* (and its unforgettable soundtrack). The movie follows the career of Olympic runner, Eric Liddell, in the 1924 Olympics.[31] Liddell was a Christian who was involved in missions with his sister. One of my favorite scenes from the movie is when Eric explains to his sister that he has decided to run in the Olympics instead of returning to the mission field. He says to her, "I believe God made me for a purpose, but He also made me fast. And when I run, I feel His pleasure."[32]

Now that is someone who knows his purpose. Liddell had a clear view of what he was made to do; his purpose was evident.

How about you? Is your purpose evident? Is it obvious what you intend to do?

Concentrated Effort

The "how" of purpose is not always an easy thing. It is not always seen by others, and sometimes it is not extremely pleasant. Look at verse 25:

> *"Every athlete exercises self-control in all things..."*
> 1 Corinthians 9:25

In the NIV, it says,

> *"Everyone who competes in the games goes into strict training."*

Strict training. Ugh! Those words do not sound like fun to me at all. It sounds hard! That is not why people sign up!

---

[31] http://www.ericliddell.org
[32] http://www.imdb.com/title/tt0082158/quotes

In twenty years of coaching, I never had anyone come to me and say, "Hey, Coach Holloway, could I come to your tryout week just for the exercise?"

You may not understand what tryout week was like. Let me explain. Tryout week, or "selection week" as I liked to call it, was when all the people interested in playing on the basketball team came to the court to show us what they could do. We did running, shooting, and dribbling drills; basically it was a week of intense workouts. It was not easy. It was not pretty. The sole purpose of tryout week was to weed out the wimps. I wanted all the potential players to know that I, the coach, was serious, and I wanted to know if they were too. Could they handle it? So we made sure the way to the bathroom was clear, in case if at some point anyone needed to...you know, feel better. Tryout week was not pleasant, but it was necessary.

This is not something you want to be a part of unless your purpose is to make the team. An athlete wanting to participate in the Isthmian Games must have been able to prove that he had trained for a solid year. Why would anyone want to do that for an entire year unless they had a clear purpose for it? The "strict training" was necessary. Not easy, but necessary.

I am afraid that in our world today we know little of "strict training." I am not sure we are in strict training for anything. In our culture, if it is uncomfortable, if it is not what we want, if it is hard work—we have an aversion to it. If we do not like it, we will do something else. If it is too much work, we do not do it, or we try to find the easy way out. Look for a loophole. Get out of it somehow. Give an excuse if it will help you. Do not work too hard. Relax! This is what we are told, and frankly, we see it all around us.

But we are not called to a life of comfort. We are called into strict training and self-control.

> *"Every athlete exercises self-control in all things..."*
> 1 Corinthians 9:25

We are called to mind renewal and living sacrifices:

> *"¹I appeal to you therefore, brothers, by the mercies of God, to present your bodies as a living sacrifice, holy and acceptable to God, which is your spiritual worship. ²Do not be conformed to this world, but be transformed by the renewal of your mind, that by testing you may discern what is the will of God, what is good and acceptable and perfect."* Romans 12:1–2

We are called to love:

> *"³⁴A new commandment I give to you, that you love one another: just as I have loved you, you also are to love one another. ³⁵By this all people will know that you are my disciples, if you have love for one another."* John 13:34–35

We are called to a higher walk:

> *"I therefore, a prisoner for the Lord, urge you to walk in a manner worthy of the calling to which you have been called."* Ephesians 4:1

Strict training. Not easy, but necessary.

Tips for Strict Training
If you were to come to my office, you would find on my shelves books on how to train physically. I have guides for weight lifting, running, and healthy eating among other subjects. I suppose it comes with the Physical Education professor territory. It is helpful to find some tips for training

when you are just starting out, need encouragement to continue, or even to find new methods to aid your progress.

I want to help you start thinking about strict spiritual training.

Tip #1: Strict training requires knowledge of what you need to do. You need to have some idea of where to start and what to do. A runner who is training for a marathon does not train by learning how to fast-pitch a softball. Of course not; that is silly. She knows exactly what to do: start running. Well, I have good news for you. All of the instructions on what to do in strict spiritual training are found in God's Word. We have the knowledge right at our fingertips. Open it up, study it, and then do what it says.

Tip #2: Strict training requires a commitment to following protocol despite the cost. You need to understand that there will be sacrifices to make, and prices to be paid. To follow the analogy, that runner training for a marathon understands that she might have to give up some of her favorite desserts or get up earlier to run every morning. That is costly, but she made the commitment to follow that training protocol. Spiritual training protocol can be found—you guessed it—in God's Word. It holds the expectations of one pursuing the glory of God. Open it, study it, and then do what it says.

Tip #3: Strict training needs a coach. Every person who trains for the Olympics has a coach. Every team working toward a championship, from little league baseball to the pros, has a coach. The runner training for a marathon likely has a coach or a training group. A coach is someone who is trustworthy. She keeps you on task, holds you accountable, challenges you, asks you good, even hard, questions. A coach is someone who encourages you. Find a coach, a mentor, for your spiritual training. Find someone who is older and wiser who will do these things for you, and then let her do it. Listen to her, and do what she says.

Tip #4: Strict training requires that you get rid of harmful things. The marathon trainer gets rid of what will hinder her in the race. Smoking cigarettes will harm the runner's lungs, and her breathing will be too labored to endure the 26.2-mile run, so she gets rid of them. She gets rid of junk food, of shoes that will give her blisters on her feet, and of heavy clothes that will weigh her down. In spiritual training, you must trim from your life things that are harming you, things that are outside your "fences." Get rid of them; they are no good. They will only hold you back and you will only be frustrated and hurt by them. You know what they are. Find them and cut them loose.

So...are you running with purpose?

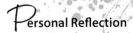

Personal Reflection

What kind of purpose has been driving your passion?

How have your ideas of "purpose" changed after reading this chapter?

How can you "make God look good" in every area of your life: at your job, in your home, to your husband, to your kids, in your ministry?

What kind of costs have you had to pay for your "strict training"?

Who is coaching you in your strict training, and whom are you coaching?

What are the things in your life that you need to get rid of so that you can run with purpose? How will you do this?

Chapter 9

Just Gotta Do Today

Without it, this book would not be in your hands.

I would have never finished writing it. I may never have even finished studying for it. Or thinking through the passage. Or reading through the passage!

I may never have received my high school, college, or graduate school diplomas. I may never have even learned to read without this quality.

Have you guessed it yet?

Persistence. Without persistence, nothing would ever get done, especially if it is a challenging task. Believe me, each thing mentioned above was a challenging task!

We are adding persistence to the list of qualities that passion—and really living—requires. Passion needs persistence.

Perseverance. Diligence. Endurance. Determination. Steadfastness. Dedication. Commitment. Even the term stick-to-itiveness (yes, it is a real word) can be found in association with persistence.

The Isthmian Games athletes sure needed persistence when they were in their training year! How many times have you set New Year's resolutions for yourself only to realize they have gone missing by March? Can you imagine how much will power and determination those athletes had to keep going for that entire year? They had to keep at it despite bad weather. They pushed just one more mile when they were not feeling well. They said "no" to their favorite sweet just because of their goal. Just because it was important enough to keep going. If they were not able to prove they had trained for a solid year, they would have been unqualified to compete in the games.

Persistence to Stay In the Game

Qualification was not important only in pre-Games training, though. Each event had regulations that the competitors had to follow. A broken regulation may result in disqualification. The prefix dis- refers to a removal of a particular property. In this case, disqualification implies that at one point the athlete was indeed qualified, but because of her choices or actions, that condition was taken away. Disqualification.

> *"An athlete is not crowned unless he competes according to the rules."* 2 Timothy 2:5

The athletes were required to play by the rules. A broken rule would take him or her out of the event. The athletes would have to be familiar with the rules in order to follow them. She would have had to know what she could and could not do when it came to the event she was participating in. But when it came right down to it, even if she did not know the rule existed, she was still expected to follow it.

It is not about winning the race; it is about running well.

It was simple: The athlete that won the event was one that had followed every rule. If you did not follow the rules, you could not be a winner. You would be disqualified for the event, and consequently for the prize.

Paul talks about disqualification in verse 27 of our passage.

> "*23I do it all for the sake of the gospel, that I may share with them in its blessings. 24Do you not know that in a race all the runners run, but only one receives the prize? So run that you may obtain it. 25Every athlete exercises self-control in all things. They do it to receive a perishable wreath, but we an imperishable. 26So I do not run aimlessly; I do not box as one beating the air. 27But I discipline my body and keep it under control, lest after preaching to others I myself should be disqualified.*" 1 Corinthians 9:23–27

But Paul's thoughts here revolve around the manner in which we run: how the race is run. He says, in summary, "I have to watch that I do not disqualify myself. I must run carefully, purposefully, and with self-control, so I do not do something that could make me disqualified."

It is not about winning the race; it is about running well. In our culture, we put so much importance and emphasis on performance, success, and accomplishment. Our society does not care how you get there, just as long as you are there and you look good. This is selfishness, and it is sin. As a result of this performance and success mindset, we have seen an increase in cheating, plagiarism, fraud, embezzlement, and deception.

Recently, former mayor of Detroit, Kwame Kilpatrick, was tried and found guilty on 24 counts including bribery, mail fraud, tax evasion, and perjury.[33] He now sits in jail, and he is not alone. There are many other examples I could give you just from reading the local paper this week. But it is not just in politics. Former Tour de France winner and founder of the Livestrong Foundation, Lance Armstrong, recently confessed to a decade of lying about taking steroids while competing

---

[33] http://www.nytimes.com/2013/03/12/us/kwame-kilpatrick-ex-mayor-of-detroit-convicted-in-corruption-case.html?_r=0

in cycling races.[34] Talk about a performance and success mindset—not only did he use steroids to ensure victory (which was cheating), but then he lied about it so that he still looked good. As a result, Armstrong has been banned from competing in any sports.

These two men have been disqualified from their positions in life. They bought into the performance, success, and selfishness-driven mindset. Now they are unable to really live.

This isn't the last time Paul talks about disqualification in his letters. It shows up again in 2 Timothy and in Titus:

> *"...so these men also oppose the truth, men corrupted in mind and disqualified regarding the faith."*
> 2 Timothy 3:8

> *"They profess to know God, but they deny Him by their works. They are detestable, disobedient, unfit for any good work."* Titus 1:16

If you do not run carefully and watch where you are going or what you are doing, you could do something that could take you out of the race. It could disqualify you for ministry. It could ruin your reputation and keep people from listening to your message. Some message blockers could include: an immoral relationship with your boyfriend, fiancée, or someone other than your spouse; lying on taxes or insurance documents; gossiping and how you talk about or to others; unkind treatment of your spouse and family; filthy language or dirty jokes; and the list goes on. These are things that could diminish or even eliminate a positive impact we have on the world around us. You could be disqualified from ministry or even blessing.

---

[34] http://www.bbc.co.uk/sport/0/cycling/21087593

It is not just the big mistakes that can take you out of the game. It could be a mindset that distracts you from what is most important. Think about it. As I said earlier, we have become very aware of accomplishment; not just getting awards or receiving a promotion at work, but even just in getting through our "to-do" list for the day. Our focus and passion can be directed toward the accomplishment of our agenda so much that we miss opportunities God brings into our lives every day. In this sense we are "disqualified" because we have changed from living for God's purpose and in His plan to living for our own checklist.

Disqualification can happen on different levels. But let me be clear: you cannot disqualify yourself from salvation. Salvation is a done deal. It can never be taken away. Jesus assured us of this fact:

> *"For this is the will of my Father, that everyone who looks on the Son and believes in Him should have eternal life, and I will raise him up on the last day."* John 6:40

> *"28I give them eternal life, and they will never perish and no one will snatch them out of my hand. 29My Father, who has given them to me, is greater than all, and no one is able to snatch them out of the Father's hand. 30I and the Father are one."* John 10:28–30

> *"11And this is the testimony, that God gave us eternal life, and this life is in His Son. 12Whoever has the Son has life; whoever does not have the Son of God does not have life. 13I write these things to you who believe in the name of the Son of God that you may know that you have eternal life."* 1 John 5:11–13

Furthermore, there's nothing you can do to put yourself outside of God's love:

> "*38For I am sure that neither death nor life, nor angels nor rulers, nor things present nor things to come, nor powers, 39nor height nor depth, nor anything else in all creation, will be able to separate us from the love of God in Christ Jesus our Lord.*"
> Romans 8:38–39

Rest well in the fact that there is nothing you can do to disqualify yourself from God's love or His salvation. Oh, what a love!

To carry the athletic example, think of it this way: an athlete in the Isthmian Games who violated a rule in an event was still considered an athlete. Maybe she stepped on the line while running, or dropped the baton in the exchange, or went outside the boundaries. But the rule violation did not somehow make her no longer an athlete. She still trains, competes, and is truly talented when it comes to athletic events. But for this specific competition, the Isthmian Games, she was not allowed to participate, or permitted to receive the prize, because of that rule violation. It is the same idea with us. If we know Christ and have accepted His salvation, then no matter what we do, we are still Christians; we cannot change that. But our actions or wrong choices may prohibit or limit us from engaging in a certain ministry, task, or even receiving the blessing.

Perhaps I should state it this way: your position in God's love and salvation can never be changed, but your ability and effectiveness in a ministry can be. Maybe you should read that one more time: your position in God's love and salvation can never be changed, but your ability and effectiveness in a ministry can be. This is the disqualification Paul is talking about.

Know truth: you cannot be disowned by God or do anything that would make Him withhold His love from you.

To be honest, as much as I try to follow the rules, sometimes I blow it. I make a mistake, I loose my temper, I say things that I should not, I react in a way that is uncalled for. It happens in my life too many times and I am guessing it happens in yours as well. But you must know this: when you make mistakes, there is life after disqualification. God forgives completely and wholly. His forgiveness keeps you in right standing with Him. The forgiveness that God gives without reservation is true and eternal. You will make mistakes, and sometimes those mistakes are big and can come with big consequences. But God heals completely, and maybe He will even restore your relationships for further impact or your ability to minister. Being disqualified is not the end of the world.

Before we go any further, take a moment to evaluate your race. How are you running? Are you running carefully, persistently, within your parameters? Run carefully, be alert, know the regulations of the race. Do not take yourself out of the event.

But if you have, know that God's forgiveness is greater than any mistake. Claim it for yourself and get back in the race.

Unfinished Art

If you are a do-it-yourself kind of person, you have no doubt seen some of the programs on television that show people building or starting projects on their own. Some of these stories on TV or in the magazines show situations people find themselves in because they have great ideas for renovations, but they just do not finish. They start all these projects but never actually get them done. The intentions were good at the start, but the lack of diligence to see it through caused more harm than good for themselves and many times, to others.

I think sometimes we have a tendency to look at our lives the same way. We mistakenly think that somehow we are a project that has just been left hanging. "God started this and made a mess, and now what am I going to do?"

Know truth: He is not done! And He is not leaving until He is done! You may be unfinished art for now, but there will come a day when you will be the finished, whole person He wants you to be. His purpose is to complete you. It is God who is doing the work in you and He will finish you!

> "And I am sure of this, that He who began a good work in you will bring it to completion at the day of Jesus Christ." Philippians 1:6

> "...But I am not ashamed, for I know whom I have believed, and I am convinced that He is able to guard until that Day what has been entrusted to me." 2 Timothy 1:12

The same grace we met in Ephesians 2 is with us for the race, too. His grace is at work in your life. His grace gives you the ability to have endurance—persistence—to live the life He has called you to. Your persistence is grace-based, not ability-based. What a freeing concept! Rely on His grace to help you run the race, and remember always that you are not alone. He will complete you!

> It is God who is doing the work in you and He will finish you!

Get Back Up Again

Sometimes life knocks you down, especially if you are a Bozo Bop Bag. Remember those? Bozo the Clown was a popular kids television program in the 1950s and 1960s. Later, in the 1960s, the Bozo Bop Bag—a punching bag—came out for kids to play with. The unique thing about this toy was that it was weighted and rounded at the bottom. It stood about four feet tall, so when you hit it, it would pop back up, and you could keep punching it over and over again.

I always wanted a Bozo Bop Bag, not because I was a violent child, but because it was fun! You could hit it, and it would get back up again. You would hit it again and again and again, and it would keep popping back up!

Persistence carries the idea of continuing on despite hard times, to keep going and to remain true to your purpose in the midst of trials. This is not a foreign concept in the Scriptures. Take a look at James:

> "²Count it all joy, my brothers, when you meet trials of various kinds, ³for you know that the testing of your faith produces steadfastness. ⁴And let steadfastness have its full effect, that you may be perfect and complete, lacking in nothing." James 1:2–4

That word steadfastness is not a word we often use in our speech these days. Some may think it old fashioned. But the word has the idea of being determined, resolute, unwavering, and relentless. Steadfastness is closely related to persistence. Steadfastness keeps me committed; persistence keeps me going forward.

You are guaranteed hard times in life; that is the hard truth. What James is saying is that these trials, when responded to with persistence and steadfastness, will actually make us stronger. But we have to get back up again.

What I am saying is that we should all be Bozos. Wait: that did not come out right. Let me try again. The Bozo Bop Bag gives us an idea of what we are supposed to do in life. We have to get back up again. We will get knocked down, hopefully not punched down, but at least knocked down.

We will have friends betray us; businesses will collapse; lies will spread; jobs laid off from; and love rejected. We are going to get knocked down. Sometimes we find ourselves down because of our own mistakes: a bad financial decision, a hastily made commitment, a compromise of convictions, or even a moral failure. Sometimes it is because of other's mistakes, or even sin. But, like Bozo, we have to get up again. Hold on to what you know to be true; remain steadfast, and go again!

This is persistence.

But you cannot have persistence without a purpose. Persistence needs a reason to get back up again. There is something you are working for, and that is what drives you to get back up. Your purpose is that thing inside of you that says, "You can't give up now! Get up, try again! God loves you, and His grace is able!" Your persistence is driven by your purpose.

> *Hold on to what you know to be true; remain steadfast, and go again!*

Have you ever watched a baby learn to walk? It is inspiring, if you ask me. A baby, usually around a year old, will see her purpose—getting to Mom's arms—and start the journey. She stands, steadies herself, and takes a step or two, and then falls down. Maybe hard. She might even cry a bit. But then, realizing her purpose again, she stands up and tries again. Nothing is going to stop her from getting to Mom. She falls down again but gets back up and takes a few more steps.

You were there once, too. But you probably do not remember that process. Think about some other things in life that need persistence. How about earning a college degree? Even the best students will admit they had some tough classes along the way. Or a morning they overslept. Or a night where they did not sleep at all while getting homework done! Sometimes failed exams or even failed classes litter the trail to the diploma. But in order to graduate, you must get up after a failed class and try again. It takes determination and persistence to walk across the stage and get that diploma. Your purpose is that diploma, and it represents four years of hard work—persistence.

Live In the Moment
There is one more thing you need to know about persistence, and we have to go back to the passage to see it.

> *"[23]I do it all for the sake of the gospel, that I may share with them in its blessings. [24]Do you not know that in a race all the runners run, but only one receives the prize? So run that you may obtain it. [25]Every athlete exercises self-control in all things. They do it to receive a perishable wreath, but we an imperishable. [26]So I do not run aimlessly; I do not box as one beating the air. [27]But I discipline my body and keep it under control, lest after preaching to others I myself should be disqualified."* 1 Corinthians 9:23–27

Persistence is a moment-by-moment thing, constantly putting forth effort and energy to complete the task at hand. Persistence doesn't worry about future or dwell on the past.

The word *race* used in verse 24 is actually the Greek word *stadion*, a word of measurement. A *stadion* measures to about 600 feet.[35] (In case you are wondering, we get our word stadium from this root.)

Six hundred feet is not very long. That is less than half a lap of a running track. This is a short race, but one that is run with intensity. As I mentioned earlier in the chapter, the emphasis

---

[35] http://www.blueletterbible.org/lang/lexicon/lexicon.cfm?Strongs=G4712&t=KJV

here is not on the distance of the race we run but on how the race is run. Persistence is needed even for 600 feet. (Ever noticed that it does not take very long for your legs to start burning when you are running?). A 600-foot race is done with constant, high level effort. There are no jogging laps or walking sections. Paul wants his readers to understand that life involves constant effort. Persistence—to keep after it, to keep fighting, to work hard—is how you are supposed to run the race.

You cannot allow difficulties, past failures, or future unknowns deter you from living in the moment. It is not about the end result. It is not about winning. It is about running right now. God never requires you to determine the end result. He only asks that you do what He has put in front of you with your whole heart, knowing that He has all the details under control.

You just gotta do today. Do not worry about yesterday. Do not worry about tomorrow. Think about today. Do today. Run today. Play the moment. Be persistent. Get back up again. You just gotta do today.

Personal Reflection

What does it mean to you to know that you cannot ever be disqualified from God's love and salvation?

What are some potential disqualifiers in your life?

What is one thing you could do this week to keep you from being disqualified?

On a scale of 1–10 (10 being best), how would you rate the intensity level of your running?

What is the hardest thing about being persistent for you?

What are some things or thoughts in your life currently that keep you from "living the moment"?

What one thing will you do this week to help you be persistent, stay on-task, and "live the moment" in your life's reality?

Chapter 10

Playing Your Trump Card

What do the television shows *Cops* and *The Bachelor* have in common? Okay, okay, you are right; they **are** both TV shows. What else?

The theme of both of these reality TV shows is essentially the same: pursuit. The cops are chasing the bad guys. The bachelor is chasing marriage. They both have specific goals and are doing everything they can to reach those goals.

They are in pursuit. They work hard to get done what needs to be done. Everything they do is for a reason, because they are pursuing that end goal.

While the Apostle Paul *was* a bachelor, we know that marriage was not what he was pursuing. He was not pursuing bad guys, either. But we do know that he was in pursuit:

> *"[23]I do it all for the sake of the gospel, that I may share with them in its blessings. [24]Do you not know that in a race all the runners run, but only one receives the prize? So run that you may obtain it. [25]Every athlete exercises self-control in all things. They do it to receive a perishable wreath, but we an imperishable. [26]So I do not run aimlessly; I do not box as one beating the air. [27]But I discipline my body and keep it under control, lest after preaching to others I myself should be disqualified."* 1 Corinthians 9:23–27

Paul says "I do not run aimlessly; I do not box as one beating the air..." He says he is running with a specific goal in mind, not running just to run. He is in pursuit.

Paul was not chasing after a wreath to put on his head, but he knew his readers would understand what he was talking about. The victor in a race or contest, like those of the Isthmian Games, was awarded a crown or prize which, many times, was a garland of leaves for her head. The Christian does not work toward a prize that will rot or become brittle in just a few days like the wreath of an athlete. Rather, we are to run after those things which have an eternal value. As Peter says, our reward is "an inheritance that is imperishable, undefiled, and unfading, kept in heaven for you" (1 Peter 1:4). The Christian pursues a prize from Jesus Christ that will last for eternity. It will not rot, or be burned; its value cannot be counted. As you live each day with a Jesus-centered perspective, you are doing what Jesus told His disciples in Matthew 6:20, "lay up treasures in heaven…" Collecting all those treasures doesn't happen by mistake. You have to pursue them.

In order to really live with passion, purpose, and persistence, there has to be a pursuit. You have to move toward the goal, chase after it, keep it in your sights. If that is true, then it is also true that pursuit carries with it the idea of intentionality. When you are in pursuit of something or someone, you do everything for a reason. A boy in pursuit of a girl sends chocolate to her because he wants to win her heart. He has done so intentionally so that he might one day soon call her his wife. His goal dictates his actions. Likewise, an athlete trains intentionally, eats intentionally, even sleeps intentionally because he is pursuing that ultimate award. Your pursuit should be characterized by intentional living. Everything you do should help you accomplish your goal in some way.

No Loitering

Have you ever seen someone run aimlessly? It is pretty funny looking. You can tell they have absolutely no idea what they are doing or where they are going; and they obviously do not know how they look, because they look rather silly! They are not running intentionally. They are not training for a marathon or running from a bear (two very good reasons to be running), they are just running aimlessly. They are not in pursuit of anything, and their actions are not intentional.

I have seen this happen a lot, actually. It always makes me laugh a bit when I see it. Any teacher will tell you, it is important to give good instructions. What makes them "good" is that they not only tell you what is going to happen, but you know when it should happen. As a professor in the Physical Education department, (and I have seen this to be true in coaching) it is important to help our students (future teachers!) learn how to give good instructions. Rule number one in instruction giving: you always have to say when before you say what. For example, if I just say, "I want you to get a ball and a partner," invariably, the students will begin moving before knowing what they should do with the ball or where to go with it. They all just start walking. They wander around with no idea where they are going or what the point is. They are not moving intentionally. So I have to say, "When I say 'go,' get a ball and a partner and line up." When they find out what the exercise or drill is, they can move intentionally, making sure they do the drill correctly.

Really living means that you cannot "run aimlessly." Wandering is not an option. It requires pursuit, and pursuit requires intentional actions. It starts with your passion. Because of your passion, purpose, and persistence, you must pursue the things that will aid each of those qualities. You have to make right choices.

Does this "making right choices" thing sound familiar at all? It should. We talked about it in chapter four. It is possible to make right choices because of God's grace. If you want to keep running with purpose and in pursuit—not aimlessly—you have to make right choices.

I want this book to be practical, not just theoretical. So here is where you get to do some brainstorming with me. What are some right choices you can intentionally make to aid you in your pursuit?

Write down some right choices here.

Here are some I thought of:

Pray. Communication is important in all of life. Communication on the basketball court is necessary so that everyone is running the same play. In a relationship, communication enables two people to know what the other's desires, disappointments, and needs are. Prayer is our communication with God. It is not just a life-line when we are in desperate need (although it is that at times). Talking with God is a necessity and, admittedly, is sometimes hard because we cannot see Him like we can see our best friend when we meet for coffee. But He is there, and He is listening. Being intentional about prayer is a good decision because it keeps us in tune with God. It reminds me that I am dependent on Him as I talk with Him. It helps me remember who He is and that I should keep my perspective centered on His desires rather than my own.

Listen. Part of communication is not just talking, but listening. When was the last time you simply sat in God's presence and listened to Him? I am not talking about hearing an audible voice. But when you are quiet and attentive in the presence of God, the Holy Spirit can move; He may bring to your mind Scripture, or biblical truths to simply remind you of His character or even use the portion of the Word you are reading to give you guidance in decision-making. Are you listening to Him?

Get in the Word. If you want to do what is right, you must first know what is right. Look no further than God's Word. If you want to follow the Holy Spirit, and if you want to walk with God, you must read and understand what He has said. It is in the Scriptures that He has revealed Himself and His desires. Getting in the Word every day is a good choice. Through the Scriptures, allow the Holy Spirit to help you understand where you need to grow or even affirm your current direction.

It is possible to make right choices because of God's grace.

Obey the Word. If you are in the Word every day, you know what is right. Now comes the hard part: you actually have to do it. Obey what you read in God's Word. *That* is a good choice!

Seek Wise Counsel. One of the most beautiful and strategic parts of the Body of Christ is that there are Christians of all ages and maturity levels. Find someone you can turn to for sound advice. Find someone older and more experienced and ask her what she did or would do in your situation; find someone who knows the Word of God and can share its truths with you.

Being intentional with what you do and making right choices are part of the pursuit. It is necessary that you live each day deliberately, doing only the things that will help you in your passion, purpose, persistence, and pursuit.

We have seen that our culture does not promote intentional living very well. Our culture preaches the mantra, "If it feels good, do it." Just doing something because it feels good is not being intentional or responsible. Plan your steps. Do things because it helps you reach your goal—fulfill your purpose— not just because it feels good. Move because you know where you are going and what you are doing, not aimlessly. Be intentional about what you do!

I mentioned previously that I spent twenty years as the women's basketball head coach at the college where I teach. God was so gracious to give me twenty years. As a coach, it was important to me to help the young women pursue team goals, but also to understand and follow what God would have for each of them to do. Sometimes God helps us teach things by asking us to do them first. Late in my coaching career, it

> *We need something that at the end of the day, it wins.*

became evident to me that God was asking me to step away from my head coaching position. I did not have a reason why, or a new position to move into. There was not a new ministry or task on the horizon, but I knew He wanted me to stop coaching. In the beginning weeks of that last year, I sat down with the team to tell them. I explained that what the coaching staff had always told them—to follow Jesus, no matter what—was what I needed to do. I could not encourage them to love God and pursue Him if I was not willing to do it myself. That afternoon was, without a doubt, the hardest thing I have ever had to do. I still have a "video" in my mind of their reactions. There were many tears, but we all took a step in our pursuit that day, determined to follow God, no matter what.

Be intentional. Make good choices; do things that aid you in your pursuit. Now you may be asking, "In my pursuit of what?" That's a good question. It is one that *you* have to answer.

Trump Wins

I do not know if you play card games, but if you do, you may be familiar with the term "trump." Some card games that use trump are Rook, Euchre, and Pinochle. Trump refers to a particular suit in the card game that will win every round or "trick" if it is played. If the trump suit is, say, hearts, then for that round any card, low or high, in the suit of hearts will beat any other card. So if you play a three of hearts, it would beat a king of clubs, and you win that round. Trump wins every time.

I like to think about the idea of having trump in the context of life. We need trump. We need something that at the end of the day, it wins. Trump is what you are pursuing. Trump is that thing that you are working for. You are running with persistence because of that trump. It is what you can look to as the most important thing.

We need trump because at some point, we are going to get pushed off course. We are going to get knocked down, and we may lose steam in our pursuit. In hard times, when you want to let go and give up the pursuit, there has to be something in you that is important, that wins every time.

As I write this, we are in the middle of March Madness, the national championship tournament for NCAA (college) basketball. It starts with 68 teams, and they play one another until there are only two left. One of these two will claim the NCAA Championship title for the season. It is called "March Madness" because it starts in March, and games are played daily. Sometimes it seems like basketball chaos. For almost three weeks, there seems to always be a game to watch, and if your husband or significant other is a basketball fan, you might have a hard time pulling him away from it. Or if you enjoy this season as much as I do, you may find yourself in front of the TV more than you should (but that's beside the point!).

Some of these teams have been knocked down during the season. It is rare that a college basketball team goes into the March Madness playoffs as an undefeated team. They have experienced a defeat, a setback to their ultimate goal. But you will not find them walking off the court and giving up after a tough loss. Why? Because every team that plays in the NCAA tournament has a trump card. The Championship title is what they play for. It is their trump card. Every time during the season that a team loses a game, they pull out their trump card, the NCAA Championship title, and keep playing. They get back up, throw on their jerseys, tie their shoes, step back on the court, and play as hard as ever. That NCAA Championship is what is important to them. It is trump, and it wins every time.

Maybe your trump is your spouse or family. When you get discouraged, you remember them, and they keep you going. Maybe it is your ministry. Let's be honest—church life can sometimes get messy, and it makes you want to quit. But because of the relationships you have built within that ministry, you get up and keep moving. Maybe your trump card is your lifelong dream; when you get discouraged about your place in life, you think about your goal or dream job and keep going to work toward it.

What is trump in you? What is that thing that is so important to you that wins every time? You have to make the decision on what your trump is going to be. Find something that you can claim as what makes you get back up after a loss. Because when hard times come (and they *will* come) you must have something that you can look to and say, "This is trump. *This* wins."

Oh, What a Life!

Let's take one last look at that passage. Reflect on what we have read and studied, allowing the Holy Spirit to move in your heart and mind using the Scriptures. Take some time to process, and write down any thoughts, underline, circle, or high-light as you feel led.

> *"²³I do it all for the sake of the gospel, that I may share with them in its blessings. ²⁴Do you not know that in a race all the runners run, but only one receives the prize? So run that you may obtain it. ²⁵Every athlete exercises self-control in all things. They do it to receive a perishable wreath, but we an imperishable. ²⁶So I do not run aimlessly; I do not box as one beating the air. ²⁷But I discipline my body and keep it under control, lest after preaching to others I myself should be disqualified."* 1 Corinthians 9:23–27

There is a lot of passion packed into those few verses. You may not be an athlete (and that is okay), but you have to pay attention to how you are running, and what you are running for. What is your passion? Keep a fixed eye on your purpose, and run with persistence. Train hard, run well, and do not give up. Do not get disqualified, and keep your trump card ready to play.

We started in Ephesians 2 and discovered the many ways God's grace is given to us. We found the wonder and awe of it: His salvation, His kindness, His power, and His unconditional, no-flowers-needed love. *Oh, what a love!*

God's love—His unconditional and extravagant kindness, benevolence, goodwill, charity—is your ultimate trump card. It is what gives you the ability to live. Because of His love, God makes you alive in Jesus Christ and equips you with the grace and skill for good works, and the ability to live a full, abundant life. All of that is because of His love. It is indescribably amazing! His love truly is the *only* reason for living!

Because of the immense love of God, we can live with incredible freedom! God offers us a life that is more than we can imagine. His life is greater, fuller, and more exciting than what our culture has to offer. We find freedom in 1 Corinthians 9 to live with passion, purpose, persistence, and finally, with pursuit. *Oh, what a Life!*

His love truly is the only reason for living!

So no matter what is going on with you right now: maybe you are in a season of waiting, or your future is unclear. Maybe you are frustrated with your job, your ministry, or marriage, or maybe it is just that the van is not running right. Maybe you have just begun a new chapter in your life, and you are excited for what is ahead. Whatever it is, whip out that trump card and *you go, girl!*

We *can* live...for the love of God.

Personal Reflection

What are some right choices that you made this week to help you in your pursuit?

What three things can you do this week to live more intentionally?

Who can you find from whom to seek wise counsel?

How is life for you right now? What tone would you use to say, "Oh what a life"?

In the midst of whatever your life's reality is, what do you know to be true about God?

What words would you use to describe your "pursuit"?

What words would you want others to use to describe your "pursuit"?

What is your trump card? Take a moment and write it out here.

Afterthoughts

Well there it is—my motivation as the only reason for truly living. There is nothing greater than the love of God! When you grasp what that truly means and what He did, *real living—the* power we need to live every day—is possible. The love of God (your trump card) gives you the power to *really live* every day. The trick is to keep that in mind. Let's face it, life (in lots of aspects) happens at an overwhelming pace these days, and it is easy to lose track of what we hold as truly important. Let me encourage you with the reality that living with God's love as your trump card is possible. There are times when you will struggle, but do not let that stop you. Refocus and go again.

I have found that having something visual is a great tool to help me remember. Whether it is a quote or verse taped to my bathroom mirror, a memento from a recent event, a note from a friend, or a little figurine that reminds me not to take myself too seriously, the visual regularly reminds me of the truth it represents. Whenever I see a daisy, I remember that *I am loved,* and I do not need to ask the flower about it! Let me encourage you to get a little daisy (I recommend an artificial one unless you have real daisies year round!) and place it in a location (maybe several?) where you will see it. Make sure it is in a prominent place...maybe even in your Bible. It is okay if other people see it. In fact, that may be even better because it will give you an opportunity to explain the love of God and the life hope you have because of Jesus.

I hope you have been encouraged by reading this book, but even more, I hope you have been encouraged by reading God's Word. Keep at it. Read it every day. This is where God has revealed Himself and tells us about His plan. This is where you will find hope and help in order to *really live.* God uses His Word to tell us about Himself and His plan; He uses it to change us, and I do not know about you, but I need a lot of changing! As I read the Scriptures and God's Spirit çseen in you, too, as all of us make *Him* look good to others.

Livin' in the Overflow,

Sherrie

About the Author

Sherrie Holloway is a gifted communicator of God's Word and is committed to teaching the truth of the Word and allowing God's Spirit to use it in the lives of its hearers. She enjoys helping those to whom she is speaking see His Word in a fresh way. It is the Word that changes people, nothing else. Sherrie shares from the overflow in her own life as she speaks with a desire that her listeners would find the overflow of Jesus in their own hearts.

Sherrie speaks to a diversity of groups through her itinerate speaking ministry, and uses each opportunity to teach God's Word in a way that is straight forward, challenging, and easy to understand.

A native of the Philadelphia (PA) area, she enjoys the beach, chicken cheese steaks, and Philly soft pretzels! The aunt of 17 nieces and nephews, she loves any time spent with her family. A member of the Baptist Bible College (PA) faculty since 1986, Sherrie has seen God do amazing things in her own life as well as the lives of those she has coached, taught, and mentored. It is her desire to intentionally and fully LIVE life, and to provide refreshment from God's Word that will allow others to live in the overflow of what God is doing.

Checkout **www.wellspringoverflow.com** to see some of what God is doing in Sherrie's life and to learn more about Wellspring Overflow Ministries.

For the Love of God

152